LATOUR FOR ARCHITECTS

Bruno Latour is one of the leading figures in Social Sciences today, but his contributions are also widely recognised in the arts. His theories 'flourished' in the 1980s in the aftermath of the structuralism wave and generated new concepts and methodologies for the understanding of the social. In the past decade, Latour and his Actor-Network Theory (ANT) have gained popularity among researchers in the field of architecture.

Latour for Architects is the first introduction to the key concepts and ideas of Bruno Latour that are relevant to architects. First, the book discusses critically how specific methods and insights from his philosophy can inspire new thinking in architecture and design pedagogy. Second, it explores examples from architectural practice and urban design, and reviews recent attempts to extend the methods of ANT into the fields of architectural and urban studies. Third, the book advocates an ANT-inspired approach to architecture, and examines how its methodological insights can trace new research avenues in the field, reflecting meticulously on its epistemological offerings.

Drawing on many lively examples from the world of architectural practice, the book makes a compelling argument about the agency of architectural design and the role architects can play in re-ordering the world we live in. Following Latour's philosophy offers a new way to handle all the objects of human and nonhuman collective life, to re-examine the role of matter in design practice, and to redefine the forms of social, political and ethical associations that bind us together in cities.

Albena Yaneva is Professor of Architectural Theory at the University of Manchester, UK. She is the author of several books, including *Crafting History: Archiving and the Quest for Architectural Legacy* (2020) and *The New Architecture of Science: Learning from Graphene* (2020), co-authored with Sir Kostya S. Novoselov. Her work has been translated into nine languages. Yaneva is the recipient of the RIBA President's award for outstanding research.

Thinkers for Architects

Series Editor: Adam Sharr, Newcastle University, UK

Editorial Board:
Jonathan A. Hale, University of Nottingham, UK
Hilde Heynen, KU Leuven, Netherlands
David Leatherbarrow, University of Pennsylvania, USA

Architects have often looked to philosophers and theorists from beyond the discipline for design inspiration or in search of a critical framework for practice. This original series offers quick, clear introductions to key thinkers who have written about architecture and whose work can yield insights for designers.

'Each unintimidatingly slim book makes sense of the subjects' complex theories.'
Building Design

'... a valuable addition to any studio space or computer lab.'
Architectural Record

'... a creditable attempt to present their subjects in a useful way.'
Architectural Review

Lefebvre for Architects
Nathaniel Coleman

Peirce for Architects
Richard Coyne

Virilio for Architects
John Armitage

Baudrillard for Architects
Francesco Proto

Merleau-Ponty for Architects
Jonathan Hale

Freud for Architects
John Abell

Kant for Architects
Diane Morgan

Latour for Architects
Albena Yaneva

For more information about this series, please visit: https://www.routledge.com/Thinkers-for-Architects/book-series/THINKARCH

THINKERS FOR ARCHITECTS

Latour
for
Architects

Albena Yaneva

LONDON AND NEW YORK

First published 2022
by Routledge
4 Park Square, Milton Park, Abingdon, Oxon OX14 4RN

and by Routledge
605 Third Avenue, New York, NY 10158

Routledge is an imprint of the Taylor & Francis Group, an informa business

© 2022 Albena Yaneva

The right of Albena Yaneva to be identified as author of this work has been asserted in accordance with sections 77 and 78 of the Copyright, Designs and Patents Act 1988.

The Open Access version of this book, available at www.taylorfrancis.com, has been made available under a Creative Commons Attribution-Non Commercial-No Derivatives 4.0 license.

Trademark notice: Product or corporate names may be trademarks or registered trademarks, and are used only for identification and explanation without intent to infringe.

British Library Cataloguing-in-Publication Data
A catalogue record for this book is available from the British Library

Library of Congress Cataloging-in-Publication Data
Names: Yaneva, Albena, author.
Title: Latour for architects / Albena Yaneva.
Description: Abingdon, Oxon; New York: Routledge, 2022. |
  Series: Thinkers for architects | Includes bibliographical references and index.
Identifiers: LCCN 2021043936 (print) | LCCN 2021043937 (ebook) |
  ISBN 9780367348618 (hardback) | ISBN 9780367348632 (paperback) |
  ISBN 9780429328510 (ebook)
Subjects: LCSH: Latour, Bruno. | Architecture—Philosophy.
Classification: LCC B2430.L3594 Y36 2022 (print) | LCC B2430.L3594 (ebook) |
  DDC 720.1—dc23
LC record available at https://lccn.loc.gov/2021043936
LC ebook record available at https://lccn.loc.gov/2021043937

ISBN: 978-0-367-34861-8 (hbk)
ISBN: 978-0-367-34863-2 (pbk)
ISBN: 978-0-429-32851-0 (ebk)

DOI: 10.4324/9780429328510

For Ilian and Kristina

'... there is always a little bit of philosophy in architecture and a lot of architecture in philosophy.'

(Latour 2005a: 70)

Contents

List of illustrations	ix
Series editor's preface	x
Acknowledgements	xii

1. Introduction: 'In this world' — 1

2. Rethinking the Modern Constitution — 5

    Are we modern? 7
    The promises of symmetrical anthropology 13
    Non-modern architects 16

3. Science in the making — 20

    Matters of facts as end product 21
    Hot and cold science 24
    Discoveries: the diffusion and the translation models 30
    Speaking scientifically, speaking legally 36
    Mapping controversies 39

4. How technology shapes everyday life — 43

    A socio-technical approach to mundane artefacts 43
    Projects and failure 57

5. Actor-Network Theory — 63

    Society or the making of the social 64
    An ANT approach to architecture 73

6. Space and spacing   79

   Process and the construction of space 80
   Spacing 82

7. Invisible cities   88

   Paris for millions 88
   Traversing 89
   Proportioning 97
   Distributing 99
   Allowing 101
   How to study invisible cities? 102

8. The parliament of things   105

   Object-oriented politics 107
   Cosmos and cosmopolitics 109
   Cosmopolitical design 111

9. A Gaia who cares   115

   The intrusion of Gaia 115
   Architectural contributions to Gaia-graphy 120

   Further reading   125
   Bibliography   127
   Index   138

List of illustrations

2.1 The Modern Constitution 7
2.2 Purification and translation 9
2.3 The two Great Divides 14
3.1 The double-faced Janus 25
3.2 Diffusion and translation model 31
3.3 Mapping controversies in architecture 41
4.1 The Berlin key 44
4.2 Key controversy 47
4.3 Networks of practices 59
4.4 Locus of enquiry 60
5.1 Plasma 72
6.1 Spacing 84
7.1 Oligoptical versions of Paris 92
8.1 The political model with two houses; The model of the collective 111
9.1 Modernisation front between global and local 118
9.2 A visualisation of the Critical Zone 122
9.3 DESIGN EARTH, 'Frozen Record', Of Oil and Ice 123

Series editor's preface

Adam Sharr

Architects have often looked to thinkers in philosophy and theory for design ideas, or in search of a critical framework for practice. Yet architects and students of architecture can struggle to navigate thinkers' writings. It can be daunting to approach original texts with little appreciation of their contexts. And existing introductions seldom explore a thinker's architectural material in any detail. This original series offers clear, quick and accurate introductions to key thinkers who have written about architecture. Each book summarises what a thinker has to offer for architects. It locates their architectural thinking in the body of their work, introduces significant books and essays, helps to decode terms and provides quick reference for further reading. If you find philosophical and theoretical writing about architecture difficult, or just don't know where to begin, this series will be indispensable.

Books in the *Thinkers for Architects* series come out of architecture. They pursue architectural modes of understanding, aiming to introduce a thinker to an architectural audience. Each thinker has a unique and distinctive ethos, and the structure of each book derives from the character at its focus. The thinkers explored are prodigious writers and any short introduction can only address a fraction of their work. Each author – an architect or an architectural critic – has focused on a selection of a thinker's writings which they judge most relevant to designers and interpreters of architecture. Inevitably, much will be left out.

These books will be the first point of reference, rather than the last word, about a particular thinker for architects. It is hoped that they will encourage you to read further, offering an incentive to delve deeper into the original writings of the thinker at stake.

The *Thinkers for Architects* series has proved highly successful over more than a decade, expanding now to eighteen volumes dealing with familiar cultural figures whose writings have influenced architectural designers, critics and commentators in distinctive and important ways. Books explore the work of: Gilles Deleuze and Felix Guattari; Martin Heidegger; Luce Irigaray; Homi Bhabha; Pierre Bourdieu; Walter Benjamin; Jacques Derrida; Hans-Georg Gadamer, Michael Foucault, Nelson Goodman, Henri Lefebvre, Paul Virilio, Maurice Merleau-Ponty, Immanuel Kant, Charles Sanders Peirce, Jean Baudrillard, Sigmund Freud and now Bruno Latour. The series continues to expand, addressing an increasingly rich diversity of thinkers who have something to say to architects.

Adam Sharr is Professor of Architecture at Newcastle University, Editor-in-Chief of *arq: Architectural Research Quarterly*, a Cambridge University Press international architecture journal, and he practices with Design Office. His books published by Routledge include *Heidegger for Architects* and *Reading Architecture and Culture*.

Acknowledgements

As a young student of sociology in 1996 I enrolled in the DEA (Diplôme D'Etudes Approfondies/Master of Advanced Studies) programme in Sociology at the *Ecole des Hautes Etudes en Sciences Sociales*, where Pierre Bourdieu was teaching. Bourdieu and his first collaborators were the key protagonists of 'Critical Sociology', an influential twentieth-century Marxist sociological tradition which flourished since the 1960s. Shortly after I enrolled in Bourdieu's seminars, I stumbled upon Bruno Latour's book *The Pasteurization of France* – an eventful read that flipped my intellectual world upside down. Following that, I abandoned Bourdieu for Latour and began my PhD at the *Ecole des Mines*, took part in Latour's doctoral seminar for 4 years, and later collaborated with him on several projects. The 'Pragmatist Sociology' developed by Latour, his collaborators (Michel Callon, Luc Boltanski, Laurant Thévenot) and their students was born in the 1980s in the aftermath of the structuralist wave in French thought. It was influenced by the work of Michel Serres, Gabriel Tarde, Gilles Deleuze, William James, John Dewey, Etienne Souriau, Harold Garfinkel, among others, and provided a realist, pragmatist perspective to study social phenomena.

Embarking into the world of architectural research in 2001, I engaged in 'translating' Latourian thinking into architectural scholarship and pedagogy. Thus, in many ways, I started 'writing' this book a long time ago. Meanwhile, Latour's work has not lost the freshness and the thrill of provocation that dazzled me as a student back then and now is dazzling my students from different disciplines. It continues to be relevant as it offers powerful interpretations of the world that we live in.

The Manchester Architecture Research Group (MARG) at the University of Manchester Urban Institute provided a stimulating intellectual environment for writing this book. I am particularly indebted to my colleagues Stephen Walker, Léa-Catherine Szacka and Kim Förster for careful reading of the manuscript and helpful comments. My PhD students – true Latourians! – Alexandra Arènes,

Brett Mommersteeg, Benjamin Blackwell, Simon Mitchell, Demetra Kourri and Fadi Shayya – contributed enormously to this book through their incredible commitment to Latourian scholarship in the field of architecture. Special thanks to Alexandra for creating the illustrations.

Adam Sharr, series editor at Routledge, provided generous comments and precious editorial suggestions. The professionalism of Fran Ford and Trudy Varcianna at Routledge did not cease to impress me. My family, Martin, Christian, and Svet were patent, again, and supportive as ever. My 16-year-old nephew Ilian amazed me with his eagerness to devour masterpieces of French thought. I dedicate this book to him and to my niece Kristina.

CHAPTER 1

Introduction: 'In this world'

At the beginning of the coronavirus pandemic in 2020, the French philosopher Bruno Latour wrote an essay for AOC, an online cultural newspaper, launching an appeal to rethink aspects of our systems of production (labour, instruments, raw materials and the social structure that regulates production) in order to become 'efficient globalisation interrupters' (Latour 2020). He asked us to imagine how different the world could look if we learned from the lockdown experience during the pandemic. This essay has since been translated into more than 12 languages, demonstrating Latour's reputation, lately reported in *The Guardian*, as 'one of the most influential thinkers of our age' (Watts 2020). This most recent media appearance illustrates the original and provocative tone of Latour's social theory that tackles issues ranging from the history of modernity, studies of science and technology, innovation, creative processes, cities, political ecology, the challenges of globalisation, religion and art, as well as the ecological crisis.

Over the course of their work architects often facilitate the production of social relations and help shape societies. Therefore, knowledge in sociology (the study of social life, social change and the factors that impact human behaviour) is crucial for designers. A Latourian sociological approach is relevant to architects for a number of reasons: first, there is a growing realisation of architecture as a social practice, recognising the social nature of the outcomes of architectural production (Till 2009); second, architectural professionals increasingly question understandings and beliefs in relation to knowledge production, innovation and creativity that are commonly taken for granted; and third, there is a tendency to acknowledge the active role of objects, materials and technologies in the process of design and inhabitation (for instance the role of scale models in the design process). Therefore, it is not a coincidence that Actor-Network Theory (ANT) associated with the name of Latour, has gradually gained popularity among researchers in the fields of architecture and design studies within the past two decades.

It is not a coincidence that Actor-Network Theory (ANT) associated with the name of Latour, has gradually gained popularity among researchers in the fields of architecture and design studies within the past two decades.

The greatest advantage of Latour's sociology is that it is realistic, pragmatist (oriented around things) and remains in *this* world. It applies care, caution, and attention to understand the world by relying on 'what comes from our own hands'. Such an earthly approach can provide a useful conceptual framework for architectural scholars and practitioners to better tackle the realities of design and architecture.

Trained in philosophy, theology and anthropology in France, Latour first worked in the US and moved back to his native France in 1982 to take a position as Professor in Sociology at the *École Nationale Supérieure des Mines de Paris*, an elite engineering school, where – together with Michel Callon, Madeleine Akrich, Antoine Hennion, and others – he founded the influential *Centre de Sociologie de l'Innovation* (CSI). Seminal work on Science and Technology Studies (STS) was developed in this research centre between the 1980s and 2000s. In 2006, Latour moved to the University of *Sciences Po*, where he is currently an Emeritus professor associated with the médialab and the programme in political arts (SPEAP).

Unlike other volumes that have provided an introduction into Latour's theory as a philosopher (De Vries 2016; Harman 2009), or offered an intellectual biography of the author (Schmidgen 2014), or a comprehensive summary of his key ideas (Blok and Jensen 2011), this book aims to introduce his work to architects. It outlines key methodological insights in relation to architecture and key concepts of particular relevance to an architectural audience, of both professional architects, and architectural, design and urban scholars.

The book is organised into nine chapters. Each chapter makes three essential moves: *first*: it presents key ideas and concepts from Latour's philosophy; *second*: it deploys some of these ideas with the help of specific examples; *third*: it offers reflections on the relevance of these concepts and methods for architecture, sketching possible avenues for research and engagement with the profession. Chapter 1 introduces Bruno Latour as a thinker and the aims and the structure of the book. Chapter 2 spells out Latour's critique of modernity and provides a reflection on the meaning of 'modern' and 'nonmodern' in architecture. Chapter 3 presents the key findings from Latour's anthropology of science and how they can inform research in architectural studies. It also discusses a method for analysing and mapping architectural controversies. Chapter 4 reviews the socio-technical approach to innovation, the role of technology and objects in social life and the concept of technical failure. It also reflects on the active role of objects in design/dwelling practices. Chapter 5 introduces Actor-Network Theory as a method and elaborates on how it can be used in architectural research. Chapter 6 analyses Latour's understanding of process and introduces the concept of spacing in opposition to space. Chapter 7 offers a pragmatist agenda for the study of cities; the case of Paris is discussed at large along with the role of urban artefacts in city life. Chapter 8 scrutinises the concept of politics orientated around objects and reflects on the meaning of cosmopolitical design for architectural professionals. Chapter 9 discusses Latour's theory of the new climatic regime and a possible architectural response to climate change. The writing style, truthful to Latour, is based on careful analysis of specific examples. The illustrations are redrawn from classic diagrams and figures included in key works of Latour and are further reinterpreted architecturally for a design audience.

As demonstrated by Latour's recent reflections on the pandemic in 2020, his philosophy continues to help us reflect on the world today. It is hoped that this book will equip architectural scholars with conceptual tools to re-examine contemporary societies and will open many avenues for a pragmatist architectural endeavour, based on what architects and users do.

It is hoped that this book will equip architectural scholars with conceptual tools to re-examine contemporary societies and will open many avenues for a pragmatist architectural endeavour, based on what architects and users do.

CHAPTER 2

Rethinking the Modern Constitution

What does it mean to be modern? How do we moderns, if that's what we are, understand our place in the world? Modernity. Progress. The linear flight of time. Nature and cultures. Humans and objects. Facts and values. A controllable world. All of these are deeply rooted in modernity: understood as a historical period, as the socio-cultural practices and attitudes that arose in seventeenth-century thought and in the eighteenth-century 'Enlightenment'. A central thread that runs throughout Latour's work is questioning the foundations of modernity.

Being modern relates to how we represent ourselves as historical. 'Modern', 'modernisation' and 'modernity' are terms that suggest a sharp contrast with an archaic and continuous past. It is a break in the flow of time and yet, we continue to push forward, everything advances. This points to an asymmetry between the past and the present that is rooted in the very meaning of what it is to be 'modern'. Moreover, in the logic of modernity, history endorses the winners and forgets the losers (Latour 1995). This creates another asymmetry. Because of this double asymmetry, Latour argued, there is a fundamental uncertainty in the way we understand ourselves as moderns. This is especially clear when we are in the midst of a practice, whether it is the making of an artefact or an experiment, where it is not possible to univocally define the direction of the flow of time and we cannot always determine who the winners and the losers are.

There is a fundamental uncertainty in the way we understand ourselves as moderns. This is especially clear when we are in the midst of a practice, whether it is the making of an artefact or an experiment.

We Have Never Been Modern (1993a) offered a powerful critique of these asymmetries. In this seminal book Latour probed the powerful dualisms (divisions that separate phenomena into two parts) of nature and culture, fact and value, subject and object that are crucial for modernity and were bequeathed to us in the seventeenth century by thinkers like Robert Boyle (1627–1691) and Thomas Hobbes (1588–1679). Boyle, for instance, as a scientist, conceptualised both nature and the origin of modern experimental science as what is independent from the social world. In his laboratory, scientists were intermediaries that spoke all by themselves in the name of things or facts. Hobbes, on the other hand, as a philosopher, theorised social and political order in terms of distinctively human conflicts and agreements, which are independent of material circumstances; citizens are represented by one of their members, the Sovereign, a simple intermediary. Both Boyle and Hobbes engaged in *purifying* Nature and Society (Shapin and Schaffer 1985). Nature with a capital 'N' and Society with a capital 'S' are those stable poles that exist by themselves and are ruled by their own laws. The capital letters point to their stability. For Latour, it is this *purification* that defines what might be called the *Modern Constitution* – a separation between the scientific power charged with representing (speaking on behalf of) things and the political power charged with representing subjects (Figure 2.1). The dualisms between Nature and Society/Culture, which constitute one way in which we define ourselves as moderns, hinder our understanding of the world.

The Modern Constitution, as Latour described it, is based on four features. *First*, the belief that Nature has a superior dimension distinct from the fabric of Society, while the premoderns believe in a continuous connection between the natural and the social order. *Second*, while Nature is transcendent (outside of human activities), Society is immanent to human activities, and possesses an inherent dimension that renders citizens totally free to reconstruct it. *Third*, the separation between Nature and Society is maintained. It is claimed Society has no relation to Nature, or the object world. *Fourth*, the idea of a God, as the arbitrator of this dualism, makes it possible to confirm these separate orders.

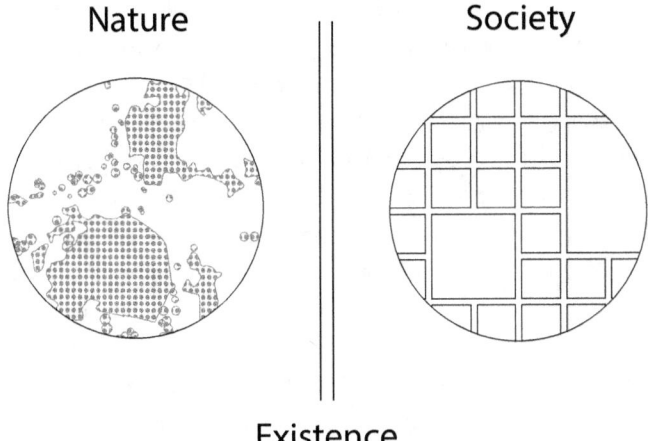

Figure 2.1 The Modern Constitution.
Illustration by Alexandra Arènes.

Here we should clarify Latour's understanding of some key terms from what he imagines is the Modern Constitution. The term Society refers to the result of the modern settlement that, for political reasons, artificially divides things between the natural and the social realms. Like Society, the idea of Nature is the result of a highly problematic settlement. This settlement, moreover, has a political origin: the separation of politics from science, of political and epistemological representation.

Are we modern?

But how is this debate about Modernity, and the divides between Nature and Society/Culture, relevant to our practice as architects? Let us take a simple example. How often do we open the pages of architectural magazines and read about controversial buildings? Every day. Here is the Disney Concert Hall designed by Frank Gehry in Los Angeles, stainless-steel, aesthetically 'beautiful' and iridescent, changing colours depending on where the sun is. Yet, it is also extremely controversial – residents and businesses complained of a blinding glare, neighbours claimed that the sunlight reflected from the building caused rises in temperatures (reaching approximately 59 °C (138 °F)), errors in construction were pointed out by the architects, budgetary constraints and the fears of earthquakes forced limestone to be replaced by steel, the tension soon escalated and the architect was sued. On the pages of *Archdaily*, we can also read about another glare dispute, this time between the Renzo Piano-designed Nasher Sculpture Centre in Dallas and the Museum Tower, a neighbouring residential building. The latter was accused of reflecting so much glare through the museum's glass roof that it risked damaging the artworks inside and making the museum's garden areas so warm that they were unusable. Similar issues of safety, temperature, respect for the neighbours and the context, clients' demands, and social responsibility emerged.

We can also follow architects at work as a building is designed in Birmingham, UK – the New Street train station. Witness with your eyes how engineers from Arup identify 'a risk of glare' for its new steel façade with a curving, non-linear complex envelope. After running further tests, both architects and engineers tackle the problem as a matter of emergency. Testing, probing, and adjusting the parameters of the sun in order to deal with the glare problem, architects consider calculations, identify areas where they have to potentially treat the steel, and analyse the amount of sun that hits the train tracks and the kind of luminosity that this creates. Further detailed tests, however, show the glare problem as a 'high risk' to blind the train drivers; and more tests and adjustments are needed. Architects consider producing camouflage patterns of different types of sanding in order to avoid the problem of glare for neighbouring buildings and the glare that could blind the train drivers and cause major disruptions at a busy train station. Yet, this elicits concerns about the 'architectural language' of the façade, the changing geometry of the envelope, and the 'radical reduction of the massing' of the building. Moreover, changes in the reflecting surface of the façade should echo the sky (blue or grey), not only the rails, and will affect the iconography of the building and the 'image of Birmingham'. An image that conveyed an important promise to citizens when the project was first presented to the public of Birmingham. Thus, the glare issue appears to be too intractable and too enmeshed in contradictory interests to separate it into purified domains. It entangles science, politics, engineering, infrastructure, economy, law, and technology. In our practices as architects, we are often mixed up in various questions of knowledge, interests, ecology, social responsibility and power; and we become scientists, artists, politicians, technologists and ecologists at the same time. In other words, hybrids.

This glare example illustrates what Latour defined as the *paradox of modernity*, and namely that modernity requires a constant work of *purifying* nature from culture, the more that purification happens and the more it attempts to prevent the production of hybrids, the more it actually creates the conditions for the growth of hybrids. By hybrid, he means complex imbroglios (entanglements) in which it is impossible to disentangle nature from culture (Figure 2.2), in the same way that it is impossible to disentangle, in the glare story above, the issues of sunlight from those of social responsibility to neighbours and other legal issues. In most contemporary situations of crisis and controversy (dispute), but also in most 'modern' practices, we encounter hybrids. Following controversies, like the

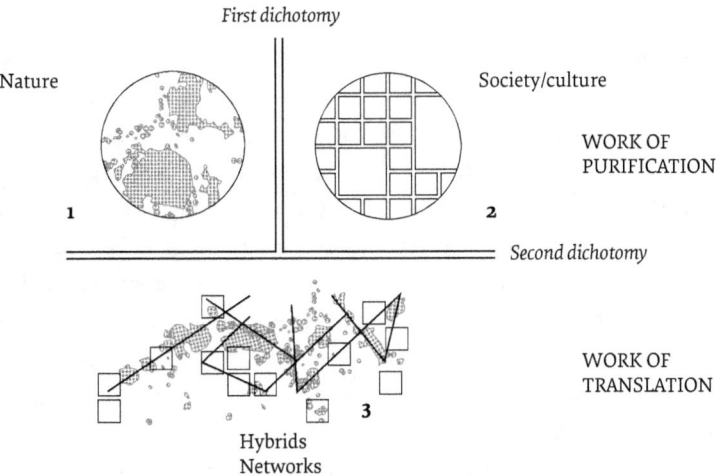

Figure 2.2 Purification and translation.
Illustration by Alexandra Arènes.

glare ones, wherever they take us, navigating through the world, we rely on the work of *translation* that draws us into hybrids, or *networks*.

In most contemporary situations of crisis and controversy (dispute), but also in most 'modern' practices, we encounter hybrids.

If we consider the two practices of *translation* and *purification* separately, we remain modern, and we subscribe to the critical project whose task is to separate them. Latour stated:

> As soon as we direct our attention simultaneously to the work of purification and the work of hybridisation, we immediately stop being wholly modern, and our future begins to change. At the same time we stop having been modern, because we become retrospectively aware that the two sets of practices have always already been at work in the historical period that is ending. Our past begins to change.
>
> (Latour 1993a, 11)

By acknowledging that many hybridisations are performed in our practice, that we are all hybrid practitioners, we stop being modern. Ensnared in the complex networks of practice, it becomes impossible to begin to distinguish what belongs to nature and what belongs to culture or society. We have never been modern and yet we have found a way of thinking that turns a blind eye to hybridisations. With this argument, at the same time original and provocative, Latour set the basis for a radically different way of understanding our world and engaged in ongoing debates about modernity and what could be called pre-modernity and postmodernity. What does he mean by these terms? Latour, on the one hand, defined *modernism* as a political settlement that resulted in a Politics in which most political activity justifies itself by referring to Nature, by pointing to the 'facts' in order to resolve debates. The glare problem above, for example, could have been resolved through references to engineering calculations and tests, but it proved to be a much more complex issue, and no expert was able to fully master the multiple forces of the sun. *Postmodernism* is a continuation of modernism, but no longer believes in its foundations. It senses that something has gone awry in the modern critique, but it is not able to do anything but prolong that same critique. The *non-modern*, by contrast, acknowledges the connections between the social and the natural order and the formation of *collectives* that foreground the political process by which these orders are brought together without dividing them into two distinct poles of Nature and Society. Again, as the glare problem shows, design practice is hybrid and operates in a non-modern way – by bringing together skies, political promises, light, engineering calculations, illumination tests, train drivers, city aspirations and architectural language into one collective.

A distinction that follows from the Nature–Society settlement is that which cuts subjects off from objects. The subject–object distinction is irrelevant according to Latour. Instead, he suggested the use of the term *nonhuman* in order to replace that of object and to widen its scope. Nonhumans can include objects, animals, divinities, technologies, regulations, and can be active participants in social life, just like subjects. In the glare story we witnessed a number of nonhumans 'acting' such as the sunlight, the engineering tests, and the Grasshopper models that probed how the surface reacts to the sun, etc. Latour's suggestion is to enrich debates about modernity by paying close attention to how the human and the nonhuman are coupled in practice; and to re-establish symmetry between them, calling for symmetrical anthropologists to foreground what he calls the work of mediation and translation. The *principle of symmetry* is crucial for his argument. It implies taking a position in the middle of events from where one can pay attention to both humans and nonhumans simultaneously, allowing for the proliferation of hybrids. This means situating ourselves, as we did, in the middle of a controversy or in the course of a design practice. From there, it becomes clear that it is impossible to artificially separate sunlight from neighbours, steel properties from budgetary and earthquake concerns, and hence why nature and culture should be treated symmetrically. An anthropology of the moderns should not limit its studies to culture (the concerns of the neighbours or the branding visions of a city), but nature (and natures) can also be studied in a similar way. Therefore, an anthropologist (or any architectural scholar) should avoid referring to social realities, power games, or other explanatory frameworks that come from outside of a controversy or design practice in order to explain what shapes reality in advance.

Referring to the political decisions or cultural branding strategies of officials in Los Angeles, Dallas or Birmingham would not explain the complex practices of architects and engineers involved in mitigating the impact of the glare. By taking the route from the middle (of a controversy or a design practice), it allows us to witness symmetrically the actions of humans and nonhumans. Where the position of moderns would be outside of a controversy or the course of events in a design practice, a non-modern position puts us right in the middle of things. Tracing different entities and following them where they lead us, we understand how they are entangled in our societies, and how the power of the sun, sunlight and glare can become a social and ethical concern for designers. As long as we follow the practices of purification, translation and mediation, we will find out that neither the modern nor the 'others' are able to separate humans from nonhumans, but they all superimpose signs and things, the natural and the social world.

An anthropologist (or any architectural scholar) should avoid referring to social realities, power games, or other explanatory frameworks that come from outside of a controversy or design practice in order to explain what shapes reality in advance.

The consequences of recognising that we had never been modern would entail the enactment of a new *Non-modern Constitution* that would no longer endeavour to purify the world along modernist lines. A notable example in that regard is the work of William Cronon (1991) who has contributed to overcome the Nature–Culture duality in urban studies. Tracing how nonhumans move back and forth between Chicago and its hinterland at the end of nineteenth century (the grain travels from the Great West farms all the way to the city markets of Chicago, the lumber travels from the Great West forests, making the forest disappear, the meat travels from the villages to Chicago, to its meat-packing corporations), Cronon showed how the boundaries of a new Nature's metropolis emerged. This city was not made by powerful men, but it took shape as it traced many intricate relationships with pine, lumber, meat, wheat, corn, and other crops, with nature. Thus, a non-modern approach foregrounds the entangled production of Nature and Society/Culture, the explicit and collective generation of hybrids. It allows us to see the composition of the world in a different way.

The promises of symmetrical anthropology

Modernity also implies another asymmetry between Cultures and their access to Nature. Another Great Divide, then, emerges from within the divide between Nature and Culture, a divide between what has been called the West and the Rest. As Latour wrote:

> **So the Internal Great Divide accounts for the External Great Divide: we are the only ones who differentiate absolutely between Nature and Culture, between Science and Society, whereas in our eyes all the others whether they are Chinese or Amerindian, Azande or Barouya – cannot really separate what is knowledge from what is Society, what is sign from what is thing, what comes from Nature as it is from what their cultures require.**
>
> (Latour 1993a, 99)

Rejecting the Modern Constitution, as that which confers power to the western scientific and industrial world, Latour stated that premodern societies are self-consciously aware of the interrelation of nature and society, a self-consciousness that is considered by moderns as paralysing. In other words, while premodern societies still confuse nature and society, moderns have managed to 'escape' from that by introducing a partition between Nature and Society (Figure 2.3)

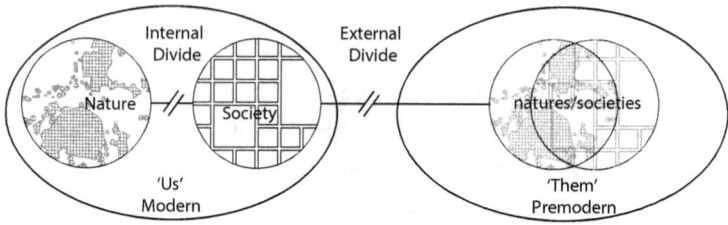

Figure 2.3 The two Great Divides.
Illustration by Alexandra Arènes.

through which they are able to distinguish themselves from those that have not yet modernised.

In addition, the notion of Culture, Latour provocatively argued, is but an artefact created by bracketing Nature out. Moderns often proclaim that there are plural cultures, many ways of being in the world, but that there is only a singular nature, only one world within which plural cultures exist. This is the foundation of what has been called cosmopolitanism and multiculturalism. In contrast to this idea of nature in the singular and cultures in the plural, Latour argued for a focus on natures-cultures. Instead of basing its findings on the comparison of cultures, a *diplomatic anthropology* should put into question both the idea of nature *and* that of culture:

> **if the unity of nature is in front of us, not behind us, then multiplicity of cultures can't be obtained by dissolving contact with a privileged point of view. None of us, I believe, would be happy to have just 'one vision among others' of the world.**
>
> (Latour 2007a, 18)

Inviting us to recognise the multiplicity of natures-cultures, Latour argued that the West and Westerners no longer exist as this one privileged Culture that grasps naked Nature. Instead of the West and the Rest distinction, there are Europeans, Indigenous peoples of North America, the Japanese, Turks,

Amerindians, as well as all the ancient cultures, to which we can add the ever-growing collection of new cultures. Each of them is in search for a home or a new place in today's globalising world. They all signal that the West, as a category, does not exist any longer. And as the Europeans had invented modernity, it is important that they are able to 'recall' it now – that is, to engage in an inquiry into what has gone wrong with modernity and to return to its founding principles. Recalling modernity for Europeans would mean that they will finally become aware of their responsibility to the cultures they have colonialised for centuries without abandoning their ambitions and will devise a new 'peace offering'. This requires professionals (scientists, engineers, architects, among others) to act as diplomats to engage in redefining and rephrasing the requirements and wishes of different peoples. Such a diplomacy will allow us all to reanalyse our own differences without referring to either the unity of Nature or the diversity of Cultures. Each culture should be allowed to express contrasts in their own terms, according to their own categories, which will enable them to resume more egalitarian relations with the 'others'.

The diplomatic and symmetrical anthropologist, *first*, tends to use the same conceptual lens to explain the true and the false, the winners and the losers; *second*, simultaneously studies the making of humans and nonhumans (the principle of general symmetry) and thus traces the generation of new beings, of 'hybrids' of nature and culture; *third*, takes a middle ground position between the traditional and new territories of studies without assuming differences between the West and other cultures that have suffered from the dominating, colonising ambitions of the West.

The symmetrical anthropologist traces the work of producing a nature or producing a society as stemming from the durable and irreversible accomplishment of the common work of humans and nonhumans as networks are built, just like we did in the glare example. She re-establishes symmetry between nature and society (the *fourth* task) to foreground the work of mediation and translation through this third middle route, allowing for the proliferation of hybrids.

<u>The symmetrical anthropologist traces the work of producing a nature or producing a society as stemming from the durable and irreversible accomplishment of the common work of humans and nonhumans.</u>

Non-modern architects

Addressing the importance of this new diplomacy, the effects of modernisation and globalisation, a historic dialogue between Bruno Latour and the architect Rem Koolhaas took place on the evening of 26 January, 2016, at the *Institut Français* in Paris, a 'Nuit des Idées' (Koolhaas and Latour 2016). These events usually bring together leading thinkers, writers, researchers and artists from around the world to engage in dialogues about the future of the planet. The discussion between the philosopher and the architect was organised around the question 'What world do we live in?' and addressed recent preoccupations of both speakers.

> Koolhaas: As an architect I have taken part in the modernisation of the world. However, as a writer I have been very critical to the process of modernisation. I agree with Bruno that the results of modernisation have been very deceitful, and we cannot continue to believe that we can create spectacular things in the future. This is a concern for everyone, a real preoccupation. [...]
>
> Latour: There is a problem in re-orienting the ambitions of modernisation and rethinking the traditional axe distributing progressism and reactionism. [...]
>
> Koolhaas: Yes, it is the first moment that we realise that something is wrong with modernisation. [...]
>
> Latour: Rem is better placed as an architect to reorient the conceptual tools of architecture towards reinventing politics today. We live in

this thin pellicle of the Earth. It is not possible to say any longer 'I will be building in the environment'. There is no environment, there is no exterior; the exterior is in the interior, the context is the content. The architects have no relation with space any longer. What will happen if we tell an architect 'You don't have the space anymore! You don't master it!' [...]

(Koolhaas and Latour 2016)

Of all the architects of his time he could have chosen to engage with, Latour picked Koolhaas, the 'never been modern' architect *par excellence*. Koolhaas's work has celebrated the energy and rigour of Modernism while also revealing its underlying controversial characteristics. His recuperation of modernity ranged from the sensuousness of Mies van der Rohe to the brute force of Russian Constructivism. Moreover, in his writings, Koolhaas considered the canonical histories of modern architecture to be mythologies (Koolhaas, 1978) and has discussed, in numerous books on the evolution of the contemporary metropolis, the consequences of modernity – endless infrastructures, neutral façades, and generic spaces. His firm OMA is, in a sense, a practice that has radically questioned modernism, redefined the social tasks promoted by classical (heroic) modernism through the amplification of the functional imagination. In each OMA project the notion of 'modern architecture' is distorted and pushed to its limits.

Latour found some resemblance between the intellectual attitude of Koolhaas and the small 'paper models' of his own philosophical urbanism: 'as a philosopher after all aspires always to render more urban the Ideal City, and that is why beyond the misunderstandings, there is always a little bit of philosophy in architecture and a lot of architecture in philosophy' (Latour 2005a, 70). As an admirer of Koolhaas's work, because it 'shocks the modernists' (Latour 2005a), Latour has scrutinised the questions of modernism and postmodernism in relation to architecture. Architects have overwhelmed us with interpretations of postmodernism, as a reaction to Modernism and the Modern Movement, criticising its dogmas, elitism and exclusivity, as well as the failure of building methods and alienating housing estates. Not only have architects spent a lot of time theorising and interpreting this movement, but more importantly, they have actually *built* postmodern buildings. However, postmodernism is, for Latour, a devalued version of modernism: we find the same arrow of time, but we start doubting its forward direction; it is full of inconsistency and nostalgia; and we can witness within postmodernism the same neglect that can be associated with anthropology as we continue to apply to ourselves the same exoticism (the quality of being exotic, strange) that we used to apply to the others. In brief, postmodernism has managed to accumulate the inconveniences of modernism without any of its advantages.

Instead of invoking postmodernism, Latour's suggestion is to suspend the two key features of modernism. *First*, instead of going from the archaic to the rational, in a steady and irreversible linear course of time from the past to the present – i.e., endorsing the idea of history as the creation of irreversible situations – the industrious arrow of time runs from one type of hybridisation to another (Figure 2.2). *Second*, anthropology is not reserved any longer to the study of 'others', but as 'we' have never been modern, it can be oriented back towards us. In the spirit of a reversed exoticism the nature of our relations in all fields of our existence – including architecture – should be submitted to a test, the results of which remain unknown. For example, phenomena like New York in the 1960s (with countless strikes, protests, and violence), Lagos in the 1990s (a dysfunctional city with burgeoning population and an infrastructure that lags behind, and a withdrawing state and planning system in decline), the Pearl River in Shanghai or Seattle in 2000s (with rapid urban expansion) cannot be explained in the strict framework of modernism. *Something happened* in these cities that defies the chronological arrow of time. These *events* – a term borrowed from the philosopher Alfred North Whitehead – have consequences for the historicity of all the ingredients of history, human and nonhuman. When made of *events*, of mediations, involving varied participants, history transforms. There is no stable 'context' that can explain the turbulent changes in these cities from outside of them. The polemic between 'context' and 'content' is a question of framing: 'a very precise repartition between what can be internalised – the architecture strictly speaking and what can be externalised – the context' (Latour 2005a, 78). This divide is a modernist fabrication. To escape modernism is also to escape the idea of a 'context', or that stable pole of Society, that is 'out there' and relied upon to explain Nature, cities, and other phenomena. Hence the importance of Koolhaas's immortal 'context stinks'. Each time we design, whether it is a library in Seattle or a skyscraper in Beijing, everything is rethought, both the 'content' and the 'context'. That is the work of translation or hybridisation. We witnessed it in the glare example where the design content of a new steel building was defined alongside the new vision of Birmingham. Everything is 'in the making'.

'Modernism', Latour claimed, 'could go forward by emancipation [liberating], the "non-modernism" (there is no exact term for this) obliges us to take seriously the key question of change of scale imposed by the simple fact that we cannot externalise any longer' (2005a, 78). It is not possible to explain any of the urban changes in New York City, Lagos, Shanghai or Seattle with contextual factors external to urban processes – that operate as external frames of explanation. To explain is to confine analysis to the 'influences' exerted 'on' Lagos or Shanghai, or to the 'social conditions' that 'accelerated' or 'slowed down' urban changes. To do so would once again be to filter the 'content' from its social environment or 'context', or to separate the vogueish steel façade with no glare from the issues of social responsibility to clients and neighbours. Yet, it is not possible to perform this filtering or externalisation because there is no context 'out there' beyond what is happening in the course of events. Instead we are all left with the work of hybridisation; a process that runs at different scales and pays close attention to the change of scale (Koolhaas et al. 1995). Like Latour, Koolhaas rethinks modernism, but with different, architectural resources. He does it so compellingly that other architects are willing to follow suit.

It is not possible to perform this filtering or externalisation because there is no context 'out there' beyond what is happening in the course of events. Instead we are all left with the work of hybridisation.

CHAPTER 3

Science in the making

Science. Technology. Society. No one has explained their intertwined reality, their dazzling undercurrents and their composite worlds – I would argue – in a more influential and thought-provoking way than Latour. In his early works *Laboratory Life* (1979), co-authored with Steve Woolgar, and *Science in Action* (1987), Latour developed an anthropology of the sciences (also called an 'anthropology of the moderns'). A number of ethnographic studies of scientific practices followed (Knorr-Cetina 1981; Lynch 1985; Pickering 1992). Ethnography is understood as the study of cultures and results in a written observational account of a particular community, society or culture and people's customs, habits, and differences. Latour's key argument is that by following scientists (and engineers) in their practices, one could witness that science, technology, and society are continually coproduced in a reciprocal and entangled process of tuning facts, theories, machines, human actors, and social relations. This argument is radical because it goes against both technological and social determinist perspectives. Technological determinism assumes that technological developments cause social change; while social determinism implies that social change is the trigger for a given technological development. Latour's work surpasses the dualist understandings that underpin such determinisms, which posit a clean split between humans and nonhumans, Nature and Society, the natural sciences and the social sciences. It equally transcends a dualist logic, in which the social sciences produce accounts of the social realm while the natural sciences strive to grasp the material world independently of human beings, social relations, and their cultural constructions of it.

By following scientists (and engineers) in their practices, one could witness that science, technology, and society are

continually coproduced in a reciprocal and entangled process of tuning facts, theories, machines, human actors, and social relations.

Matters of facts as end product

Surpassing these dualisms, *Laboratory Life* described the routine work carried out in one laboratory – the lab of Roger Guillemin at the Salk Institute for Biological Studies (1965) in La Jolla, California. Basing their findings on material gathered from *in situ* monitoring of scientists' activity, Latour and Woolgar argued that the many aspects of science depend on the routinely occurring minutiae of scientific activity. Historic events, breakthroughs, and competitions are examples of phenomena which occur over and above a continual stream of ongoing scientific activities. This approach is defined as 'anthropological' as it attempts to apprehend as 'strange' those aspects of scientific activity which are readily taken for granted. The uncritical acceptance of the concepts and terminology used by some scientists has had the effect of further enhancing the mystery that surrounds the doing of science. Attempting to demystify this activity, the authors argued that 'adequate descriptions can only result from an observer's prolonged acquaintance with behavioural phenomena. Descriptions are adequate, according to this perspective, in the sense that they emerge during the course of techniques such as participant observation' (Latour and Woolgar 1979, 37). Thus, capitalising on the experiences of ethnographic observation of the Salk laboratory *in situ*, by being close to localised scientific practices, the observer has a *situated* viewpoint from which to understand how scientists themselves produce order and how their daily activities lead to the construction of facts.

Challenging the idea that facts are things discovered by scientists that reflect an objective reality, Latour and Woolgar argued that facts are instead manifestly and socially made, they are *artefacts* constructed by scientists themselves. The distinction between 'the social' and 'the scientific' is itself an artful contrivance of scientists: a strategy they use in the social production of facts. Thus, *matters of fact* are not, as in common parlance, what is already present in the world, but a rather late outcome of a long process of negotiation and institutionalisation. They are themselves *social*. This does not limit their certainty but, on the contrary, provides all that is necessary for matters of fact to become indisputable and apparent. To be indisputable is the end point, the outcome, and therefore, not the outset, the beginning. Matters of fact do not pre-exist attempts to know them. The anthropologist observes the process of the construction of facts and the reasoning processes in science noting its similarity to common sense discourse, and thus accounts for the intense collective work required to stabilise a fact. Yet, once stabilised as facts, all traces of practices and human agency (the actions and interventions of people generating effects) involved in their production, are systematically stripped away. The facts seemingly stand on their own. In addition, scientists work not only to establish facts as facts, but also to cast doubt upon the facticity of other scientists' statements. Rather than focusing on the theories of the actors, or their place within a specific paradigm, Latour and Woolgar produced a concrete and detailed ethnographic account of how scientists behave, how they talk with one another, how they interact with their technological devices, and how facts need to travel outside of the lab in order to exist. This type of sociology of science shows that the actual practice of science is radically different from the dominant accounts of science that focus upon the public relations of science and offer idealised accounts of its theoretical structures.

While engaging in fine-grained explorations of science *in the making* to understand the cognitive and social dimensions of scientific experimentation and visualisation, and the fabrication of scientific facts, the architecture of the scientific building where the study of Latour and Woolgar unfolded remained neutral. Although the observation happened in an acclaimed building designed by Louis Khan, the Salk Institute in La Jolla, none of the aspects of its distinctive architecture and the specific interior design features appeared to matter in the account as the authors remained focused on the nitty gritty reality of fact construction. Nevertheless, intrigued by the way 'the special relation between office space and bench space is sufficient to distinguish the laboratory from other productive units' (Latour and Woolgar 1979, 47), the authors showed how the relationship between writing and research activities generated specific spatial practices that made the lab distinctive from a factory or an administrative organisation. But, this begs the question, what role does the building and the architecture of the laboratory play in scientific practices? Does it have an impact on the ways in which science is done? What about the rectangular courtyard flanked by two mirror-image concrete buildings that overlook the Pacific Ocean? Or the materials, like the 'pozzuolanic' concrete, the building's unfinished look? What about the 'generic' laboratory with wide open spaces that facilitate interactions between the scientists? Or the 'interstitial spaces' that afford flexibility within the laboratory, which is crucial to the fast-changing world of science? How does architecture and design intervene into the construction of facts? Such questions of architecture of science have become the focus of discussion between architects and science studies scholars since the 1990s (Blackwell 2022; Galison and Thompson 1999; Gieryn 2006; Novoselov and Yaneva 2020) and strengthened the synergies between the fields of science studies and architectural studies.

Inspired by Latour and Woolgar's approach to science practices, in the past two decades or so, there has been an upsurge in the number of ethnographic accounts of architectural practices (Callon 1996; Borch 2008; Farías 2015; Gottschling 2015; Houdart and Minato 2009; Jacobs and Merriman 2011; Jenkins 2002; Llach 2015; Lefebvre 2018; Rose, Degen and Mehuish 2014; Sharif 2016; Yaneva 2005, 2009a, 2009b, 2018; Yarrow 2019), engineering practices (Bucciarelli 1994; Henderson 1998; Loukissas 2012; Mommersteeg 2020; Vinck 2003) or product design (Murphy 2015). These studies investigated the culture and the practices of designers rather than their theories and ideologies. They followed *what designers do* in their daily and routine actions by prioritising the pragmatic content of actions, not of discourses. They paid close attention to *how* architects and engineers themselves produce designs and mobilise visualisations to think in a designerly way.

Hot and cold science

In *Science in Action* (1987), Latour further developed a programme for the study of scientific activities. He argued that the sociology of science should not be confused with the sociology of scientists, their careers, professions, citations. Instead of being interested in the ideology, ideas, the explanation of the errors, or the 'social aspects' of scientific truth, and instead of analysing scientific thought and spirit, Latour's agenda was to study the practices, instruments, objects, and the knots of the networks of practice, just like he did in *Laboratory Life*. That is, to pay attention to the collective, distributed and situated practices of science making.

Therefore, he advocated a *realist* approach to science studies, which consists in understanding the multiplicity of objects, places, instruments, situations, and events, and how in their totality they contribute to the manifestation of a scientific phenomenon and to the production of truth. Engaging in criticism of the regressive tendencies of critical sociology and the reflexes of anthropology, Latour defined the 'realist approach' in opposition to the 'critical approach'.

We should note here that 'Critical Sociology' flourished in French academia in the 1960s with the writings of Pierre Bourdieu. Drawing on the social theory of Karl Marx, which focused on the struggle between capitalists and the working class, this sociological method is based on critique that consists in explaining the subjective experience of all members of society with their belonging to specific social structures. The main task of critical sociology is to reveal and expose previously hidden social mechanisms and influences that impact human action. Condemning the tendency of critical sociology to reduce any human activity to social dimensions, Latour argued against a reductive definition of society. Society is, according to him, not made out of the 'social', but is also made of nonhumans, of a diversity of types of associations, that are no stranger to the social body. Thus he advocated a 'Pragmatist Sociology'. Born in the 1980s in the aftermath of the structuralist wave in French thought, this method is based on what people do, the actions they undertake and assume, their discourse (the way they explain and conceptualise what they do). It takes seriously the practices and languages of all members of society rather than searching for what social forces are 'really' acting behind them.

Engaging in criticism of the regressive tendencies of critical sociology and the reflexes of anthropology, Latour defined the 'realist approach' in opposition to the 'critical approach'.

To illustrate the juxtaposition between the two approaches, the critical and the realist/pragmatist, Latour used the double-faced Janus (Figure 3.1). On the left, stands ready-made science: it is serious (like the facial expression of the left Janus!), certain, formal and restrained, and as it is ready-made, static, and mute, it is easily explained through social dimensions; on the right, stands science 'in the making': it is alive, uncertain, informal, changing and cannot be explained with a given Society or reduced to social factors. To be understood, it needs to be followed as it is *in the making*.

Figure 3.1 The double-faced Janus.
Illustration by Alexandra Arènes.

Formulating the rules of the realist method, Latour invited us to analyse facts and technologies that are in the process of their making, that is, to follow the process through which they are *black boxed*, closed up, completed. Black boxing is an expression from the sociology of science that refers to the way in which scientific and technical work is made invisible once the final product is successful. When a machine runs efficiently, when a matter of fact is settled, no one pays attention to its internal complexity. Thus, paradoxically, the more science and technology succeed, the more opaque they become. That is why, Latour argued, we need to follow facts when they are disputed, before they become settled, cold.

In other words, we need to be there 'before the box closes'. In addition, in disagreements and controversies, where facts or technologies fail or are disputed, more and more black boxes are opened in search of a cause or explanation, and, gradually, we are led towards the conditions in which the facts were produced, we mobilise more texts and entities, and the discussion, indeed, becomes more 'scientific'. Thus, the production of facts and technology is a collective process to the extent that 'the fate of what we say and make is in later users' hands' (Latour 1987, 29) as they enter into other relations, are used in other ways, and perhaps, are disputed, or put under trial in other experiments or uses. Thus, a fact is not only socially constructed but is also 'what is collectively stabilised from the midst of controversies' (Latour 1987, 42). As the outcome of disputes, facts and technologies have a *social* life.

We need to follow facts when they are disputed, before they become settled, cold.

In addition, Latour underlined the importance to study not just the intrinsic qualities of scientific statements but to carefully account for their transformations, as well as the transformations they endure in the hands of others. Scrutinising the anatomy of scientific texts, he demonstrated the heterogeneous (varied) ingredients that constitute science in the making, both technical and social. The more something is technical and specialised, the more social it becomes: it gathers more allies and critics and by so doing increases the number of *associations*. The term *association* refers to a different regime of connecting humans and nonhumans that shape heterogeneous collectives in place of the concept of Society that exists as a substantial social body that precedes and organises what happens in social relations.

Paying close attention to laboratories as places where scientists work, Latour analysed, in particular, their instruments (or, what he has called *inscription devices*). An instrument, for him, is 'any set-up, no matter what its size, nature and cost, that provides a visual display of any sort in a scientific text' (Latour 1987, 68). An optical telescope is an instrument, but so is an array of radio-telescopes separated by thousands of kilometres. Instruments produce readings, which in turn, become *inscriptions*. An *inscription* is a general term that refers to all the types of transformations through which an entity is materialised into a sign, an archive, a document, a piece of paper, or a trace of the process of making a fact. Inscriptions are usually two-dimensional, superimposable, and combinable; they are mobile as they allow new translations of the entity in the making to happen while keeping some types of relations intact. We have witnessed some architectural inscriptions in the glare story where glare tests and Grasshopper models, drawings and calculations, luminance measures, all provided a way to trace how sun power and glare effects can travel, get translated and materialised. Inscriptions can be also called *immutable mobiles* (Latour 1987), a term that focuses on the movement of displacement and the contradictory requirements of the task. But also because inscriptions allow an entity to travel, to be displaced, without changing completely – it is *immutably* mobile.

As scientific activities unfold, one can witness an immense accumulation of ways of registering and devices of inscription. The series of visual inscriptions produced by the instruments help the scientist become the spokesperson of the phenomena that is inscribed on the screen of an instrument. The spokesperson is able to talk on behalf of a phenomenon, viruses, and other entities that do not talk on their own. Latour argued that 'in practice, there is not much difference between people and things: they both need someone to talk for them' (Latour 1987, 72). The scientist is able to be a representative of the natural world through the experimental set-up and the inscription devices that give her the power to speak on their behalf. The strength of the spokesperson of a virus comes from the fact that she does not speak on her own, but always *in the presence* of those represented.

A new object in the lab does something which is registered by the instruments which read it and produce inscriptions. This in turn becomes the basis of scientific texts. Before it becomes a thing, an endorphin, for instance, is a readable list of performances registered with the instruments in the lab. The list of actions of that object shapes its existence; it is named after what it does – i.e. TRF thyrotropin-releasing factor – as a result of local *trials* in a specific lab. Thus, in their emerging state, objects are defined by trials, by experiments of various sorts in which new performances are elicited. Defining objects by *what they do* under laboratory trials, science studies thus focus on the complex and controversial nature of what it is for them to come into existence, to act, and become actors.

However, since in English *actor* is often limited to humans, and remains anthropomorphic, Latour borrowed the term *actant* from semiotics. Semiotics is the study of activities that involve signs, where a sign is what conveys a meaning; it is generally concerned with the processes by which we comprehend or attribute meaning. Actants include nonhumans in the definition – anything is *potentially* an actor. Whoever and whatever are represented are actants. Representation is understood here in the broad sense of how language, images and objects generate meaning. The inspiration comes from the semiotician A. J. Greimas, for whom all actants do not coincide in strict terms either with the figures of the subjects or with objects or institutions in analysis of narratives, or stories. They are rather specified according to their accomplished function; they are characters, objects or animals which 'accomplish tasks, undergo tests, reach goals' in narratives (Greimas 1987, 70). An actant is thus the linguistic representation of a person, an animal, a machine. Greimas distinguished between actants, 'having to do with narrative syntax' and actors, which are 'recognisable in the particular discourse in which they are manifested' (Greimas 1987, 106). Both Greimas and Latour treated actants as relational beings that gain strength through associations with other actants. This term also designates the lack of source of agency. Action is not merely related to a particular agent or explained by enduring historical structures and systems; it rather *passes* through all actants who receive it and transmit it to others. Inspired also by Greimas's ideas of narrative analysis, is also the ability to write descriptions that let act whatever acts and show relations in their making. While Greimas restricted his analysis to literature, Latour extended it to the world itself, as a way to analyse and describe scientific and engineering practices.

Latour argued on numerous occasions that the biggest error of sociology consists in wanting to build a society with only humans and to imagine a theory of 'consensus' among humans that remains ignorant to the demands of nonhumans. However, this consensus does not allow us to explain either the sciences or the technologies because it relies on a pre-existing definition of social groups, and established rules of the game and social factors and entities commonly encountered in sociological analyses – capitalism, class struggle, nationalism, multiculturalism, gender relations – that are brought as *explanations*.

The biggest error of sociology consists in wanting to build a society with only humans and to imagine a theory of 'consensus' among humans that remains ignorant to the demands of nonhumans.

Yet, exploring *science and technology in the making* can lead to redefining the composition of social groups, and to modifying the state of things by questioning the nature of alliances and associations, and the nature of the social link between them.

> The problem of the builder of 'fact' is the same as that of the builder of 'objects': how to convince others, how to control their behaviour, how to gather sufficient resources in one place, how to have the claim or the object spread out in time and space.
>
> (Latour 1987, 131)

Following scientists and engineers at work, one can witness how they recruit and mobilise a great number of allies, most of whom do not resemble humans at all. Tracing the *trials of strength*, one can witness the specific ways a controversy is resolved (instead of its easy closure through the 'voice' of Nature). Thus, what constitutes Nature is the result of a controversy and not its judge; reality is what resists (as the Latin word *res* indicates) all efforts at modification. And it remains reality 'at least for as long as the trials of strength are not modified' (Latour 1987, 93). At a certain point, no contesting actor can modify the form of an object that is realised and gains reality in a *relational* way. Thus, no one lives in a Culture or belongs to a Society before being confronted by others; culture or society only gain a precise meaning *in the process* of a controversy and as *long as it lasts* and *according* to the force exercised by those involved.

Discoveries: the diffusion and the translation models

Drawing on the analysis of Louis Pasteur's work (Latour 1988a), Latour engaged in debunking the very notion of scientific discovery as simplistic and human-centric. That is, the assumption that everything was *there* (microbes, electrons, DNA structure, gravity, Diesel engine) and an individual found it, revealed it, discovered it, made it appear in public. One individual, in a miraculous moment of inspiration had the idea to do it. Questions of how to allocate influence, priority, and originality among great scientists, and whom to attribute the discovery have preoccupied history of science debates for a long time. The only reasonable explanation of novelty for them lies with the initiator, the one who *first* had the idea and whose genius gains mythological dimensions. Criticising this view, Latour argued that the assumption that an individual possesses ideas is absurd and the assumption that a society forms the milieu in which an idea can be developed and *diffused* is losing currency:

> the diffusion model now invents a society to account for the uneven diffusion of ideas and machines. In this model, society is simply a medium of different resistances through which ideas and machines travel.
>
> (Latour 1987, 135–136)

The belief that there is a society *out there* at a great distance from science and technology is an artefact of *the diffusion model* (Figure 3.2). In this model, society is made of social groups that have interests; these groups resist, accept or ignore both facts and machines, which have their own inertia. In consequence, we have science and technology, on one hand, and a society, on the other. This process of purification leads either to social or technical determinism. There is an expectation that Society (social factors) is capable of influencing, directing, and even shaping the course of science and technology. When something goes wrong, the appeal to Society or social factors becomes more prominent, to seek a cause or an explanation in Society or in Nature. To restore symmetry, Latour suggested that the studies of science and technology should rather start by deconstructing the concepts of 'ideas' and 'society'. It is not enough to produce a social explanation of the development of scientific or technical ideas because

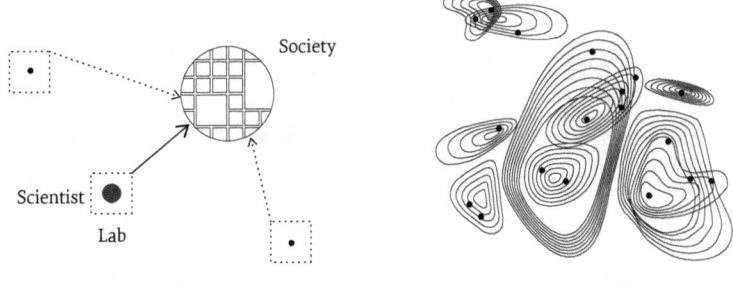

Diffusion model   Translation model

Figure 3.2 Diffusion and translation model.
Illustration by Alexandra Arènes.

> we are never confronted with science, technology and society, but with a gamut of weaker and stronger associations; thus understanding what facts and machines are is the same task as understanding who the people are.
>
> (Latour 1987, 140–141)

It is in fact this chain of heterogeneous associations, of *translations*, that we witness when we follow processes of innovation and science in the making. *Translation*, like the term inscription, is a term that criss-crosses the modernist settlement. In its linguistic and material connotations, it refers to the displacements through other actors whose mediation is indispensable for any action to occur. In place of a rigid opposition between context and content, society and technology, chains of translation refer to the work through which actors modify, displace, and translate their various and contradictory interests.

The *translation model*, in contrast to the diffusion model, asks us to acknowledge a multitude of people (not just one person, a discoverer), and to follow many scientists and engineers at work. How often do we encounter or hear them mention that they rely on social factors? Rarely do we hear them mention social classes, the forces of capitalism, the economic infrastructure, gender inequality, culture or the social impact of technology. They, themselves, do not know what society is made of, just as they are attempting to find what nature consists of:

> It is because they know about neither that they are so busy trying out new associations creating an inside world in which to work, displacing interests, negotiating facts, reshuffling groups and recruiting new allies.
>
> (Latour 1987, 142)

<u>The *translation model*, in contrast to the diffusion model, asks us to acknowledge a multitude of people (not just one person, a discoverer), and to follow many scientists and engineers at work.</u>

Following these negotiations and translations leads us to a better understanding of science in action. Thus, when the Pasteurians proposed microbes, they also offered a new and unforeseeable organisation of nature and society at the same time: a new social link. The microbes establish a new rapport between humans and animals in connecting them, associating them in a different way. Considering 'symmetrically the efforts to enrol and control human and nonhuman resources' (Latour 1987, 144) leads us to formulate *symmetrically* the same arguments about society and nature without attributing to Society any privilege. The new principle of symmetry suggested by Latour is a radical one, inviting analysts to follow and explain the closure or the opening of the controversies instead of using Society as source of explanation. The settlement of a controversy, in other words, is the cause of Society's stability, and not the reverse.

It is commonly believed that scientists inhabit an internal bubble cut off from the social factors on the outside. The divorce between society and science, and context and content, is often called the 'internal–external division'. Latour claimed that there is a danger in separating the study of the external factors in scientific activity such as budgets, political support, from the study of the internal achievements and results in science. If we follow the first series of actors, we will meet politicians, businessmen, ministers, sponsors, professors and lawyers; if we follow the second series, we will meet materials, concepts, facts, and prototypes. In this logic, the first series is necessary for the second one. The main consequence of this way of seeing, however, is that whatever we can learn about one of the series does not teach us anything about the other. This complete separation, this radical divorce between two sets of incommensurable information, shapes the internal–external debate in the sociology of science. Depending on which side we choose, we can tell two different stories; we see either scientists or politicians. Yet, this model, according to Latour, is unsustainable and its credibility doubtful. If we follow science in the making, we will be able to witness both the formation of the interested groups and the formation of chains of heterogeneous associations, of assemblages. Scientists produce both the social context and the things in the context, just as engineers produce both the market and the products in the market. The coproduction of people and things will be incomprehensible if we were to break the chains of translation with an artificial barrier establishing this divide. In contrast to the logic of the internal–external debate, following science in the making and the logic of translation, we can tell the same story, in the end, no matter if we start from the outside or the inside. Moreover, it is not a question of balancing and compromising between the contents of the laboratory or the social context, but rather about telling *one single story*.

Thus, instead of talking about Science and Technology (as ready-made), to better account for all elements related to scientific contents even if they appear less clear, unexpected or strange, Latour suggested the term *technosciences* (science in action/technology in action), always in plural. Just like the actors we follow, we *do not know* the limits, the composition and the ingredients of technosciences:

> we should be as undecided as the various actors we follow as to what technoscience is made of; to do so, every time an inside/outside division is built, we should follow the two sides simultaneously, making up a list, no matter how long and heterogeneous, of all those who do the work.
> (Latour 1987, 176)

This will allow us to understand how *they*, the actors, establish limits, boundaries, and how *they*, the actors, purify the ingredients; following the two sides simultaneously, we should be able to draw a list, as long and as heterogeneous as it might be, of all those who contribute to the work. This will lead us to follow an entire *network*. A network 'indicates that resources are concentrated in a few places – the knots and the nodes – which are connected with one another – the links and the mesh: these connections transform the scattered resources into a net that may seem to extend everywhere' (Latour 1987, 180). If, according to the diffusion model, there are only a few scientists working, debating and sharing ideas because they are unique, talented, 'superhuman', in the model of translation, if there are only a few scientists, it is because there is a *network* that prolongs their work. There are *other actors*, and missing masses, who help them, or divert them. The notion of networks helps us understand how so few actors manage to cover the world; for instance, telephone or meteorological networks could cover the entire world. The emergence of a 'society' or a 'culture' is a consequence of the construction of longer networks that make us cross paths followed by others.

The notion of networks helps us understand how so few actors manage to cover the world; for instance, telephone or meteorological networks could cover the entire world.

This, moreover, means that we have entered a relational understanding of reality. Following Latour, we must distinguish between a rationalist, a relativist, and a relational position. If *rationalists* believe in straight causal explanations that sustain *asymmetries* between cause and effect, mind and world, society and nature, *relativists* defend a *symmetrical* position that goes against the principle of explanation through social factors. *Relativism*, as a term, refers to the mundane process by which relations are established between viewpoints and the paths that allow one to move from standpoint to standpoint are multiplied. Relativists believe representations should be sorted out without independent and impartial referees. Yet, if we continue to follow scientific networks to witness what they capture in their meshes and what escapes them, we will end up with a third view, *a relational one*. Instead of being absolute relativists pleading for symmetry between perspectives or standpoints, the relational thinkers strive to find out the stronger and the weaker relations in order to establish the relative solidity of associations. They, therefore, still believe in *reality*.

Drawing on Latour's anthropology of technosciences, we can question 'How often do we witness giants, starchitects expounding ideas in the world of Architecture, making ground-breaking discoveries'? Never. Tracing architecture in the making, we instead can witness thousands of designers at work, crowds of engineers, contractors, developers and users all enrolled into a building project as well as thousands of nonhumans mobilised in architecture making (materials, technologies, models, codes, skills, different types of expertise). Yet, only a few get designated as 'heroic geniuses' (Till 2009), advancing design ideas, as bright stars in the exclusive Pritzker Prize galaxy. They are seen as *having* 'ideas' that are *diffused* into Society. Instead of focusing on the few exclusive architects, a symmetrical anthropology of architectural practices would embrace a translation model, tracing architecture in the making – like I did by following the work of OMA architects and foam models, not of one big Pritzker mind (Yaneva 2009a, 2009b) or Sophie Houdart and Chihiro Minato did in their study of Kuma Kengo's practice (2009) – to unpack the complex realities of architecture in action.

Speaking scientifically, speaking legally

Tracing comparisons with science, Latour engaged in a study of legal practices in *The Making of Law* (2010a), an ethnography of French administrative law based on shadowing judges, administrators and politicians at the *Conseil d'Etat*. Following them both in the tribunal room where the public audiences are given, but also behind the closed door where the cases are discussed, Latour offered a unique account of 'the close knitting of legal reasoning' (Latour 2010a, viii). This type of anthropological study, in a way, started back in the 1970s with the anthropology of science, technologies and markets. In this new study Latour used similar methodological principles within the context of law. An anthropology of law has the interesting feature in that – contrary to the anthropology of science – there has never been any question that all cultures *have* law. Instead of providing a social explanation of law, Latour traced the *passage*, the *transit* of law, or the path of something quite elusive that we call 'legal', that can be traced and highlighted only thanks to a detailed ethnography. Just as the first ethnography of science practices followed the construction of facts, here Latour followed the construction of legal arguments. In the same way that Latour was able to extract in *Laboratory Life*, from a limited set of case studies, a plausible definition of what it means to speak scientifically

of some states of affairs, in *The Making of Law*, through another carefully
devised set of ethnographic devices, he succeeded in extracting and highlighting
a plausible definition of what it is to speak legally. The two studies relied on the
same assumption, that the essence of science or law does not lie in a definition,
but to understand them we need to trace the situated, material practice that ties
a whole range of heterogeneous phenomena together in a certain specific way
(what we call 'scientific' or 'legal'). In the same vein of analysis 'the architectural'
can be traced and understood too (Yaneva 2010).

Following the paper trail of the dossiers circulating in the Council, Latour argued
that the only way of preventing the lawyer from interrupting the efficiency of a
decree that is contested by his clients is 'to ensure that the bond that physically
attaches the constituted authorities of the Republic to the text is not broken'
(Latour 2010a 33). He unpacked the logic of these movements and attachments,
and the specific form of continuity that allows legal arguments to travel from
one text to another. Following the slow fabrication of a file, tracing how the
cardboard folders grow and expand, fold and unfold, and pile up in cupboards,
offices, corridors, cellars, armchairs or desks, does not mean neglecting, for a
moment, the intellectual and cognitive foundations of the law. Instead, it allows
us to trace how law follows a procedure.

Just as we do not understand anything of Science if we think that words are
distant from and opposite to things, 'in the same way we do not understand
anything of Law if we seek to pass directly from the norm to the facts of the
particular case without this modest accumulation of papers of diverse origin'
(Latour 2010a, 22). Following its trail through slow description and photography,
tracing this tedious and slow step-by-step procedure is what Law *is* about: 'The
power of the Law, like that of a chain, is exactly as strong as its weakest link
and we can only detect this link by following the chain link after link, without
omitting a single one' (Latour 2010a, 90).

Following these links, in a few minutes of reasoning, of speaking legally, one
can move through political considerations, economic interests, confessions free
of prejudices, concerns about opportunity, justice, good administration, all of

which impact on, disturb and suspend the making of law. Law is thus mixed with everything, rather being a pure domain. Thus, there is no clear-cut distinction between what resembles the social and that which could be called law. The analysis of law follows the direction explored by Latour in the first studies of science and technology by abandoning the sociology of the social for that of association.

Engaging in a comparison of scientific and legal practices, Latour argued that in both practices one finds speech, facts, judgments, authorities, writing, inscriptions, all manner of recordings and archives, reference works, colleagues and disputes, but their 'distribution is at once too similar to warrant a distinction between the facts of science and the fact of law, and too different for them to be seen as a single function' (Latour 2010a, 208). One difference is striking: the so-called *libido judicandi* is very different to the *libido sciendi*. Whereas in court, judges are entirely unmoved by a case in which only the claimant is passionately engaged, the scientists in the lab can be passionately interested in scientific matters. Advocating comparisons between different constructions of the world (legal, scientific) and how they can be made comparable, now that the nature–cultures relationship no longer allows for appropriate relations to be established, Latour put a provocative argument forward: contemporary societies have to reanalyse their own differences without referring to either the unity of Nature or the diversity of Cultures. They should be allowed to express contrasts in their own terms, according to their own categories. Taking up Latour's offer of comparative anthropology, architectural ways of composing the world are yet to be explored and new studies are to be conducted to unpack what it means to speak architecturally, and what it means for all of us to know the world in an architectural way and to be connected architecturally.

<u>Contemporary societies have to reanalyse their own differences without referring to either the unity of Nature or the diversity of Cultures.</u>

Mapping controversies

Controversies are integral to many features of scientific and technological practice and dissemination. Drawing on the importance of studying controversies, as outlined since his first studies of scientific practices in the 1970s, Latour has developed a method known as 'Mapping Controversies'. The method consists in underlining what is already 'dimly discernible in the shared practices of scientists, politicians, consumers, industrialists and citizens when they engage in the numerous sociotechnological controversies we read about daily in our newspapers' (Latour 1993a, 144). As such, it operates in a more modest, down to earth mode, opposite to the mode of critique, which aims to devise a revolutionary programme of action. The methodological assumption underpinning controversies studies is that by following a controversy as it unfolds, one can learn something about the underlying social dynamics of science and technology. Controversies refer to disagreements involving all kinds of actors; none of which can be explained by reference to the social realm alone. In controversy studies, the analyst should not constrain observation to any single theory or methodology; the phenomenon should be observed from as many viewpoints and worlds as possible (Venturini 2010). Mapping is thereby a means of tracing, analysing and visualising the successive stages of controversies, the different statements of the actors, their relations and disagreements, using a variety of new representational techniques and tools. It refers to an 'art of describing' processes and practices as they unfold, by following the complexity of phenomena without replacing the specific with the general. Tracing the actors' dynamics, the spaces and times they generate, the method provides inventive narrative techniques to gain access to the particular and to grasp the unique. It aims at accounting for the performances of all participants instead of unveiling the hidden social or political meanings behind the disagreements (as this is normally done in the spirit of the critical tradition). The purpose of the maps is thus not to teach actors what they are incapable of understanding, but to learn from them how to observe their collective existences.

Drawing on the rich tradition of semiotics, mapping controversies offers a method of enquiry that questions the traditional epistemology of the social sciences. In the past decade or so, the method has also gained currency as a teaching philosophy in a number of other fields adjacent to STS. Only recently was the method introduced in English-speaking universities with Manchester (Architecture) pioneering this field along with Oxford (Geography) and MIT (Science Studies). Drawing on controversy mapping theory and previous teaching experience at the *École des Mines*, I started teaching a course on Mapping Controversies in Architecture in 2008/2009, inviting students to use their advanced design skills to draw and visualise a controversy (Figure 3.3).

Controversies in architecture, however, do not refer particularly to media debates or scandals surrounding architecture but rather to the series of uncertainties that a design project, a building, an urban plan or a construction process undergoes; a situation of disagreement among different actors over design issues, uncertain knowledge or technologies. It is a synonym of 'architecture in the making'. Following architectural controversies, we find out that the materiality of buildings is as complex as the world of their symbolic interpretations. By adding the material multiplicity to the symbolic multiplicity in architecture, a much more complex picture emerges: hence the need to map it. Following a contested design, we gain access to the social and the architectural in their fluid states. When we are in the midst of this process, we wonder: is this 'social', 'economic', 'natural', 'aesthetic' or 'technical'? If instead of rushing into classifying what we see into contextual frameworks or pre-existing categories of explanation (i.e. social, political or cultural factors), we just follow and describe, draw and map, we witness that neither a building nor a given context is static. Welsh society does not exist 'out there' behind the controversy around the design of the Senedd parliament in the 1990s, German cultural climate in 1990s Berlin cannot explain the glass dome of Norman Foster's Reichstag. Rather than taking societies, cultures and buildings for granted, we trace, map and account what architecture and society are really made of. Social, political and cultural issues are articulated by the actors themselves as a controversy unfolds. We witness many heterogeneous associations of actors that disagree, and that is precisely what gives strength to the social at the end. Thus, in the course of mapping,

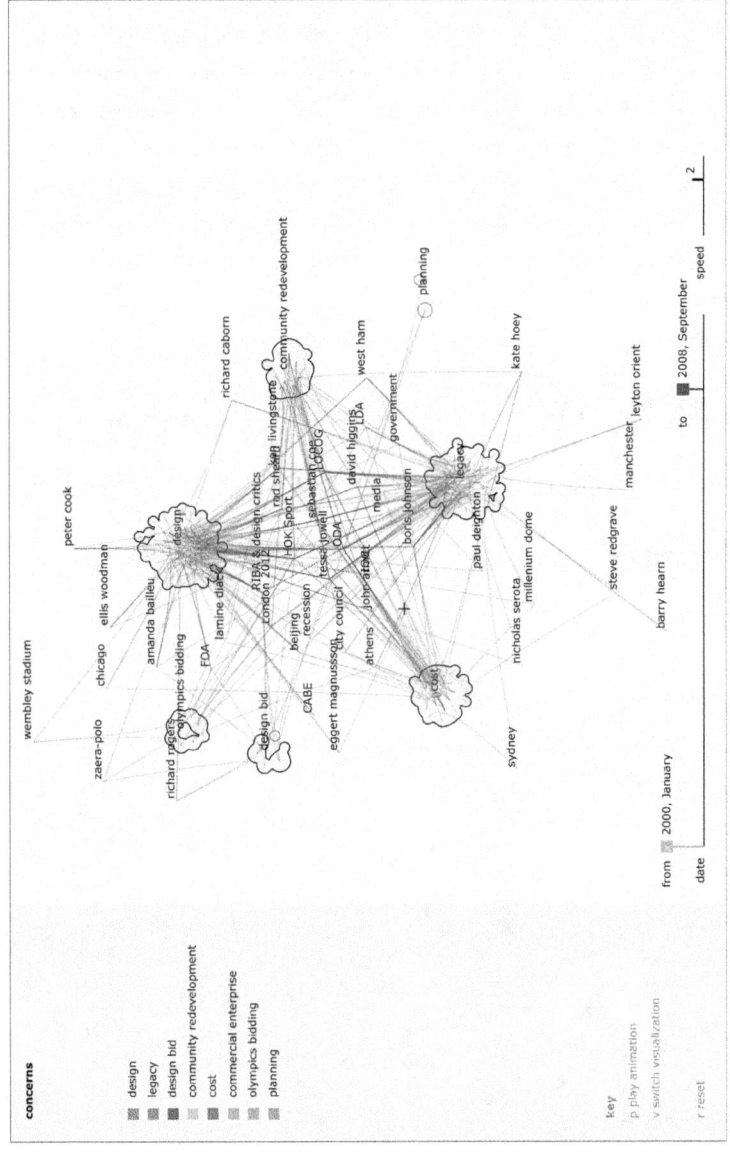

Figure 3.3 Mapping controversies in architecture.
Illustration by the author.

we will irreversibly alter the meaning of the word 'social': it is the outcome of all the trials that the actors undergo. Thus, shifting scholarly attention from the study of 'social' factors (and class struggle/nationalism/gender relations) to the study of 'associations', as per Latour's invitation, will get us closer to the complexity of architecture. Mapping controversies in architecture (Yaneva 2012, Yaneva and Heaphy 2012, Kourri 2022) is also fuelled by recent developments in computational design and can be used to produce innovative visual accounts of different architectural processes without referring to external factors. These accounts can greatly enrich the descriptive analytical techniques of architectural researchers.

<u>By adding the material multiplicity to the symbolic multiplicity in architecture, a much more complex picture emerges: hence the need to map it.</u>

CHAPTER 4

How technology shapes everyday life

Our everyday lives are constantly shaped by interactions with objects, and yet objects in our life stories tend to be told and interpreted in two ways: either through their intrinsic materiality (that would define them as real, objective and factual) or through their more aesthetic or 'symbolic' aspects (that would define them as social, subjective and lived). Latour's philosophy helps us navigate this division which is modernist in origin. In the pragmatist perspective that guides Latour's approach to objects, the divide between the 'subjective' and 'objective' is abandoned in favour of the idea of mediation. Technology plays an important role in mediating human relationships. We cannot understand societies, argued Latour, and how they work, without an understanding of technologies and how they shape our everyday life. We cannot imagine a society that is not built by things – IT technologies, trains, telegraph cables, cars, but also – we might add – buildings and infrastructure.

<u>In the pragmatist perspective that guides Latour's approach to objects, the divide between the 'subjective' and 'objective' is abandoned in favour of the idea of mediation.</u>

A socio-technical approach to mundane artefacts

In the 1980s, Latour, and his collaborators from the *Centre de Sociologie de l'Innovation* (CSI) in Paris, Madeleine Akrich and Michel Callon developed a number of what might be called socio-technical studies of innovation

(Akrich, Callon and Latour 2002; Callon 1986b). To illustrate the social dimension of technology and tackle the material aspect of societies, let us look at an iconic example from Latour – the Berlin key (Latour 1991). The Berlin key (*Schließzwangschlüssel*) is a forced-locking key for a type of door lock designed to make people close and lock their doors, usually a main entrance door or gate leading into a common yard apartment block. This wonderous surrealistic key has two identical symmetrical blades at each end rather than the usual single blade (Figure 4.1). Invented by the Berliner locksmith Johannes Schweiger at the end of nineteenth century, the Berlin key was produced by the Albert Kerfin & Co company starting in 1912. It was a solution to the problem of access via communal doors of such blocks (Lovell 2017). With the advent of more recent locking technologies, this kind of lock and key is less common.

The key is used as follows: first, you push the key in the keyhole (action 1) to unlock the door from the outside; you turn it anti-clockwise by 270° (action 2) and the door opens, inviting you to enter the courtyard of this Berlin apartment block. You think that you can quickly recover your key and enter, but you find with dismay, and eventually anger, that you cannot! You

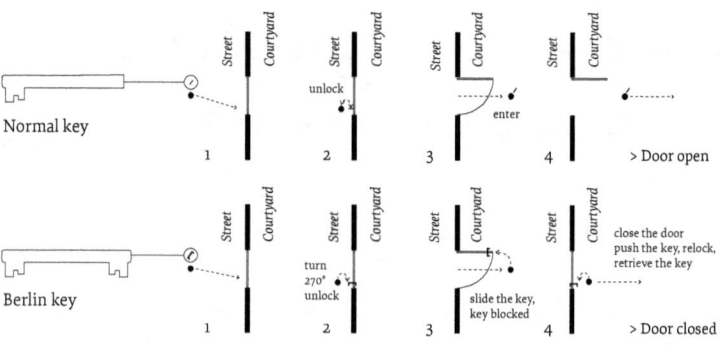

Figure 4.1 The Berlin key.
Illustration by Alexandra Arènes.

try to withdraw the key (action 3) after having bolted the door by a 270° rotation, as per the habit you have with other keys, but with the Berlin key it remains stuck within the lock. After some struggle and trial-and-error, trying to pull the key out, trying to turn it in different directions, you find out that you have to push the key through the hole, sliding it gently through the door (action 4). The key protrudes from the inside of the door, reminding you that 'it's not over'! You pull it, but the key manifests its disobedience, again. It will not come out of the keyhole; it resists your attempts to remove it. However, eventually you learn, that it is only by bolting the door on the other side of the door, on the courtyard side, that you are able to recover the key. At last, the door is closed and locked behind you, and you are finally in. This mechanism requires a tedious ritual of entry. It makes it impossible for you to forget to lock the door behind you, without also forgetting the key in the lock. It also makes it impossible to lock an open door. But, this is only how the key functions during the night. During the day it works differently; the door remains open permanently as the concierge is usually there to monitor it. The concierge has a different key. It has no groove, is thinner, and has only one bit; they can bolt and unbolt the door as they want in the usual way, just as with all keys in the world. This allows the concierge to open and close the door when needed for the delivery people, mail carrier, doctors, guests, etc.

Latour's encounter with the Berlin key happened before 1989, and before the great upheaval of the fall of the Berlin Wall (the first version of the essay on 'The Berlin key' was published in 1991). The changing socio-political climate in Berlin dominated the public imaginary of the time, begging to frame the interpretation of the unusual design technological functioning of this key. To dramatise two possible interpretations of the key, Latour engaged in an imaginary dialogue with an academic colleague, a social scientist (an archaeologist, more precisely). A possible interpretation of this distinctive key is the symbolic one. Faced with the key, we might be tempted to produce an interpretation of the symbolic meaning that would consist in saying: 'In West Berlin, before the fall of the Wall, people felt divided, they felt locked-in and threatened, so much so that they started doubling the number of doors, barriers, and even bits on their keys'. This double-sided Berlin key is just another wall built in the city, but a subtle one, as it remained invisible, hidden within a key. And we could continue this line of interpretation of the hidden meaning of German technological objects. The archaeologist would definitely endorse this interpretation. Through this lens, the key emerges as a passive, projective surface for various symbolic meanings (of social division, the political climate, fear, domination, ideology, and segregation). The key, one might say, following the archaeologist, perfectly reflects Berlin and Germany's social climate at that time. The material world is a mirror of social relations, and technology, thus nothing more than a material embodiment of discourse. The archaeologist does not see the object *itself*, but habits, behaviours, actions, meanings and symbols that can be *read* from it. The assumption embraced in this line of interpretation is that objects carry meaning, and receive and reflect it, but can never fabricate it. It is assumed that Society is made elsewhere, and with social means only (therefore, not with objects, tools, or technologies). Engaging in a critique of this explanatory framework (i.e. critical theory-informed anthropology, economy, archaeology, sociology), Latour offered an alternative way to understand technology. If, instead of unravelling the hidden meaning of objects, we follow their functioning, specific constraints, and exigencies, if we unravel the daily web of use of particular technologies, we will be able to understand how precisely they relate to society, and we will witness their 'programme of action'.

If, instead of unravelling the hidden meaning of objects, we follow their functioning, specific constraints, and exigencies, if we unravel the daily web of use of particular technologies, we will be able to understand how precisely they relate to society, and we will witness their 'programme of action'.

By *programme of action* – a term that the sociology of technology uses to give technical artefacts their active and often polemical character – Latour designated that each device anticipates what other actors, humans or nonhumans, may do. Every complicated mechanism re-inscribes contradictory specifications, every wheel and crank is a possible answer to an objection. The programme of action is in practice the answer to an *anti-programme* against which the mechanism braces itself. Devices that seek to annul, destroy, subvert and circumvent the specific programme of action of the key are called *anti-programmes*. The four actions that were needed to make the key work constitute its programme of action. However, these anticipated actions may not always occur because other actors may have different anti-programmes from the point of view of the first actor, in our case, the actor wishing to open the door and recover the key. Therefore, the key can become the front line of a controversy between *programmes* and *anti-programmes* (Figure 4.2). The concierge is working hard to prevent various anti-programmes. The thief who wishes to go through the door without a key develops an anti-programme; the resident who has twisted one of the blades of the key to make it asymmetrical so she can enter at any time is also engaging in an anti-programme. The key and the lock mediate all these complex relations

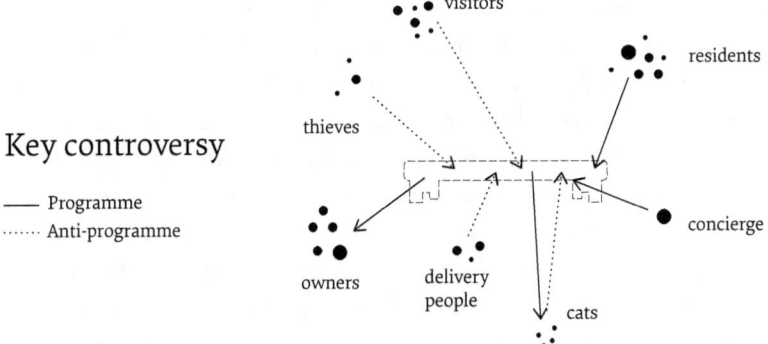

Figure 4.2 Key controversy.
Illustration by Alexandra Arènes.

between tenants and owners, inhabitants and thieves, the concierge and intruders.

Another way to describe the programme of action is through the term 'script', coined by Madeleine Akrich (1992), which designates at the same time the vision of the world incorporated in the object and the programme of action that the object is supposed to accomplish. Technologists or engineers will define the characteristics of their objects by making hypotheses about the entities that make up the world into which the object – that they are designing or testing – is to be inserted; they are exploring the object's possibilities:

> Designers thus define actors with specific tastes, competences, motives, aspirations, political prejudices, and the rest, and they assume that morality, technology, science and economy will evolve in particular ways. A large part of the work of innovators is that of *inscribing* this vision of (or prediction about) in the technical content of the new object. I will call the end product of this work, a 'script' or a 'scenario'.
>
> (Akrich 1992, 208)

Going back to the example of the Berlin key, the 'script' of the key would read: 'please, bolt the door behind you during the night and never during the day'. It has a very practical programme of action that differs from a symbolic representation of a divided Berlin. It is durably and faithfully fulfilling actions that hold Berliners together. In addition, it can hardly be replaced by words, signs, or warnings such as 'Lock the door'! that can easily be bypassed or ignored. In contrast to the fragile world of signs, the key as an object is durable and reliable. Of course, up to a point, because the key can, as we saw above, also be inserted into an anti-programme; it can be manipulated to perform other actions that may go against its original programme of action. Berlin inhabitants are not always trustworthy or reliable and are likely to diverge from a given path, and not open or close the door in the right way; they too need to be disciplined, and if they are unreliable, we can substitute the 'trust' in the people to behave correctly or follow signs, with another delegated human character whose only function is to open and close the door, the concierge. Once in place, he can filter people and exercise control with verbal warnings and tiresome reminders. Yet, to do this in a reliable manner he needs to be disciplined as well: he needs to make sure he gets to work on time, that he remains in his position watching the door, filtering people into the building. And if humans have to be constantly disciplined to be able to control and discipline other humans, the symmetrical key performs this action in a smooth and reliable way, without verbal reminders. Of course, nonhumans too can fail to regulate human actions. For instance, red lights are usually respected, at least when they are sophisticated enough to integrate traffic flows through sensors; the sign 'policeman' is often respected even though it has no whistles and body to enforce it. Social rules do not exist *on their own* but are often *delegated* to people and to things that will act on their behalf.

Taking away our attention from the world of signs and meaning, the sociology of technology developed by Akrich and Latour (1992) aims at rendering visible how technical objects (rather than simply mirroring meanings and symbols) produce modes of social, political and ethical organisation.

> **The object does not reflect the social. It does more. It transcribes and displaces the contradictory interests of people and things.**
>
> **(Latour 1992, 153)**

Thus, objects never simply adopt the political or social will, but generate a dynamic web of political, ethical or social relations. These ideas can be easily transferred into architecture where the object could be a building, a design project, a master plan. With the Berlin key, we are neither in the world of signs, nor altogether in the realm of social relations. Rather, we are in a world that is made of very specific relations, or *chains of associations*, between humans (H) (concierges, Prussian Locksmiths, know-how, skills, behaviour, and habits) and nonhumans (NH) (keyholes, steel, key, teeth, grooves, etc.). Chains of associations of humans and nonhumans (H-NH-H-NH-H-NH-H-NH) replace the absolute distinction between objects and subjects. There are only trajectories and dispatches, paths, and trails of relations to study. If we consider things, we will find humans; if we consider humans, we are by that very act interested in things. Watching carefully the actions of opening the door in that Berlin building, we witness, following Latour, that it is neither the user nor the key that unlocks a door, it is rather the chain of *mediators* that opens a door: good social behaviour *and* practical know-how *and* the concierge *and* the key lock *and* the door, all mobilised in a network.

It is neither the user nor the key that unlocks a door, it is rather the chain of *mediators* that opens a door: good social behaviour *and* practical know-how *and* the concierge *and* the key lock *and* the door, all mobilised in a network.

The term *mediator* is used to emphasise that objects are participants in the course of action that is overtaken by other *agents*. The mediator is an actor that cannot be defined by its input and its output; it always exceeds its conditions. An *intermediary*, in contrast, is fully defined by what causes it. While an intermediary is a black box that transports meaning without transformation, a mediator can transform, translate, distort, and modify meaning; it is unpredictable and does not serve as a reification of the social like many faithful and predictable intermediaries do.

If the Berlin key was studied as an intermediary, it would express, reify and reflect Berlin Society; the key would be an object *of* discourse and *of* the social, which both are made elsewhere. However, in the many entanglements of practice, in the process of opening and closing doors, the Berlin key gains the status of a mediator. This means that the social relations between residents

and owners, inhabitants and thieves, or inhabitants and delivery people are
mediated – *which is to say translated and transformed* – by the key and the
lock. The Berlin key, the door and the concierge, the inhabitants and the
external visitors are all engaged in a 'bitter struggle for control and access'
(Latour, 1991, 18). Everything changes if the object is treated as a *mediator*.
Latour wrote:

> Then, the meaning is no longer simply transported by the medium but
> in part constituted, moved, recreated, modified, in short expressed and
> betrayed. No, the asymmetrical slot of the keyhole and the key with two
> bits do not 'express', 'symbolise', 'reflect', 'reify', 'objectify', 'incarnate'
> disciplinary relations, *they make them, they form them*. The very notion of
> discipline is impracticable without steel, without the wood of the door,
> without the bolt of the lock.
>
> (Latour 1991, 19; emphasis mine)

The owners of the Berlin apartments did not manage to construct a
solid social relation based solely on verbal warnings. It became hard to
establish discipline through signs. It was difficult to enforce good social
behaviour on trust and warnings alone. A more durable set of rules and
social relations is performed through the introduction of technologies,
steel, and wood. Thus, the social needs keys and locks, argued Latour, but
also – we might add – infrastructure, buildings, designed environments,
material arrangements, furniture, and building technologies, in order to be
performed in a durable way; in other words, it cannot be constructed with
social means only.

How would this impact how we define the role of planners and architects
as those who participate in the making of social relations with architectural
and spatial means? The distinction between *intermediary* and *mediator*
in architecture studies could inform further thinking: how can we study
design and cities if a key is not a simple tool, if a door is not a simple
wooden material, if a building is not a simple construction, but that they
all rather assume the role of active mediators, of 'active form' (Easterling

2012), capable of translating, modifying, and crafting new social relations, re-shaping relational dynamics between groups, and acting as effective agents of societies and cultures? This way of thinking can most certainly lead to fruitful recalibrations of the interpretative lens of architectural history and theory as well as to changes in the operative landscapes of architectural practice (Moore and Wilson 2013) and education (Cavanagh, Verderber and Oak, 2019).

Moreover, it is important to note that engineers and designers constantly *delegate* action to nonhumans; they substitute designed objects, environments, and devices for the action of people; they add 'scripts' to the material environment. Objects are deliberately designed to constrain and shape human action by redistributing competences and prescribing responsibilities. They can replace and occupy the position of humans; we delegate the action of closing a door to hinges, springs, and hydraulic pistons, as we delegate the action of traffic control to many signs and speed bumps (or 'sleeping policemen'). Latour called *prescription* the 'behaviour imposed back onto the human by nonhuman delegates', following the analysis of Madeleine Akrich (1992). He wrote that

> **Prescription is the moral and ethical dimension of mechanisms. In spite of the constant weeping of moralists, no human is as relentlessly moral as a machine, especially if it is (she is, he is, they are) as 'user friendly' as my Macintosh computer. We have been able to delegate to nonhumans not only force as we have known it for centuries but also values, duties, and ethics. It is because of this morality that we, humans, behave so ethically, no matter how weak and wicked we feel we are.**
>
> **(Latour 2008, 157)**

The speed bumps indeed impose on humans the need to slow down, to be cautious. But this also makes us ethical beings and socially responsible citizens. The material world pushes back on us because of its physical structure and design; in addition to speed bumps, many other urban artefacts and environments mediate our lives in cities. Fences, heavy doors, bicycle covers, fountains, and barriers all prescribe behaviour: they authorise and forbid, give permission or hold promises in a dense urban context. Not passive and indifferent frames for subjective passions, but active agents contributing to the flexible networks that constitute a city.

Just like the use of the Berlin key in a divided Berlin in the 1980s, the seat belt in our cars has been delegated with a specific programme of action. It is supposed to politely make way for us when we open the door and is supposed to strap us in firmly when the door is closed. There is no escape from the belt! 'The only way not to have the seat belt on is to leave the door wide open, which is rather dangerous at high speed' (Latour 2008, 152). It imposes on us the injunction: 'Don't crash through the windshield'! which is a translation of 'Don't drive too fast! It is dangerous'! As an artefact, it takes on the (sometimes contradictory) wishes and needs of both humans and nonhumans, the car and the driver, the road and the traffic controllers. Once in the car, a sound reminds us to use the seat belt; it is impossible to start the car before you buckle it. All these measures make us disciplined, ethical drivers. It has become almost morally unbearable to see a driver without a seat belt.

To maintain order and safety on the roads, we could either discipline human drivers (with verbal warnings and instructions) and remind them to drive carefully and put their seat belt on, or delegate to nonhumans and technology this very function (the ergonomic design of the car, door signals, the impossibility of starting the engine as well as numerous urban artefacts and road signals). Here again, the technical delegation is more reliable than the verbal warning, which can easily be forgotten or overlooked. Moreover, where the belt has to strap us firmly inside the car but also, in case of accident, it should be able to be easily unbuckled to get out of a crashed car. The designer has the difficult task to make sure to 're-inscribe' all these contradictory usages, to think simultaneously of the programme of action and any possible anti-programmes.

Translated into architecture, designers plan for all different kinds of uses and misuses of their buildings and designed environments, and anticipate, when possible, various anti-programmes. Architects know well how important it is to factor in that possible gap between the prescribed user and the actual user (Hill 2003; Cupers 2013). They are also fully aware that there are many possible anti-programmes and that their buildings will be used in surprising ways. They know how difficult it is to accommodate and fit together the many contradictory demands and desires of the many different groups that are involved in the making and designing of buildings, a colossal task that, when successful, will result in good buildings and smart spatial solutions.

Going back to the discussion on mundane artefacts, it is important to note that a seat belt does not prevent the car from crashing, just as a key does not open a door on its own. It is the trading-off and the distribution of competences between humans and nonhumans (H-NH-H-NH-H-NH-H-NH) that opens a door or disciplines a body in the front seat of a car. And that is why the divide between objects (keys, belts, buildings) and subjects (concierges, car drivers, inhabitants) is untenable; this distinction is engraved in the fracture of action. As Latour reiterated, it is absurd to believe that society is made of human relationships *only* (and that the social is always made out of the social) and that technologies are made of nonhuman relations *only*. What we witness in practice, as we follow the mundane actions of seat belts and doors, speed bumps and barriers, is this reciprocal relationship between humans and nonhumans.

What we witness in practice, as we follow the mundane actions of seat belts and doors, speed bumps and barriers, is this reciprocal relationship between humans and nonhumans.

If the power of things is much more effective than the power of words, as Latour suggested, what does this mean for the things produced by designers and architects? A Latourian sociology of mundane artefacts inspires us to think of the capacity of the built environment to replace and shape human action. If mundane objects and large-scale technologies can mould the decisions we make, influence the effects of our actions, and change the way we move through the world, so do buildings, infrastructure and various urban environments. Thus, following Latour, we can state that we cannot understand how a society works without appreciating how design shapes, conditions, facilitates, and makes possible everyday sociality (Yaneva 2017). Drawing on the understanding that matter is absorbed into meaning (Albertsen and Dicken 2004; Crawshaw 2021; Hennion and Dubuisson 1996; Yaneva 1997, 2001; Yaneva and Hennion 2000), that design is *in the world* as the terms *programme of action*, *script* and *prescription* imply, architectural studies could engage in scrutinising how materiality from one side, and morality, ethics, politics, from the other, coalesce in design.

When it comes to analysing the question of *agency* (the power to act, to 'do' things with a purpose), some clarifications are needed. *First*, agency is not initiated by a specific subject or by a specific object (neither the seat belt nor the driver starts the action of fastening a seat belt). It rather *emerges* and is performed by the collective of H-NH (seat belt and diver, concierge and key). In the heat of action, the subject is decentred as many other actors take part; all agents per-form each other in that process of shaping the collective. *Second*, agency is not related to the intentional and reflexive action of humans. Often, we have the tendency to attribute agency to humans who have intentions. Instead, agency, for Latour, differs from strategic, wilful intention, but expresses itself in fragmented actions. It is related to the different parts of the hybrid collective and subsequently to the different arrangements of materials and people (H-NH-H-NH-H-NH-H-NH). *Third*, one has the tendency to attribute agency to a single person or a specific localised point that does not move. However, agency can be possessed by a field or a process that moves and travels progressively. Agency is distributed, not localisable. *Fourth*, there is a tendency to distinguish between the world and words, but the text and the context shape each other mutually. What matters is the chain of translations between things, texts, people. Machines, objects, people and texts resist, act and react, they cannot be reduced to language. It is precisely the movements of resistance and translation that matter and tell more than the words on their own are capable of saying. Thus, agency is nonstrategic, distributed and decentred (Callon and Law 1995).

Accounting for the agency of buildings (just like Latour did it for mundane artefacts) would mean witnessing what buildings do and grasping their pragmatic meaning (Kärrholm 2012; Yaneva 2009a) rather than employing an analytical frame of mind. If we follow, for instance, dwelling as it unfolds, we witness that users do not stand for social forces, or symbolically represent order or divisions of labour, but that they *perform the social* as they dwell and connect to each other (Bouzarovski 2015; Jacobs, Cairns and Strebel, 2007; Rose, Degen and Basdas 2010; Strebel 2011; Yaneva 2009a). They all remain linked through design. A socio-technical perspective to design cuts across the subjective–objective dichotomy. Mobilising this approach in architectural studies can lead to explorations of the simultaneous genesis of buildings and their environments, and to do justice to the many material dimensions of things without limiting them in advance to pure material properties or to social symbols.

In this way, a Latourian approach also offers a powerful way of resolving the dichotomy between technological determinism (that technology shapes society) and social constructivism (that society shapes technology). Although Latour agreed with the social constructivist claim that socio-technical systems are developed through negotiations between people, institutions, and organisations, he took a step further to argue that artefacts are part of these negotiations. Their behaviour often has a comparable role to that of humans (although they cannot act and feel like humans). If artefacts can be deliberately designed to both replace human action and to constrain and shape the actions of other humans, how can built form, infrastructure and design environments shape human action? How can designers 'act at a distance' through the buildings they create, and how, from a user's perspective, can a design environment appear to compel certain actions and impede others? Latour's sociology of mundane artefacts inspires us to address all these questions, to scrutinise the relationship between producers, built environments, and users, and to analyse how certain values and social goals can be achieved through specific design techniques.

Projects and failure

Shifting the socio-technical analysis from the scale of mundane artefacts, such as the Berlin key or the seat belt, to complex technological systems, Latour has studied the development of the iconic Personal Rapid Transportation (PRT) project Aramis, a high-tech automated subway system. That is also a shift, we must note, from the analysis of objects to that of *projects*. The great advantage of technology studies is that they deal with projects that are obviously neither objects nor subjects nor any combination of the two. Latour analysed the Aramis innovation as it wended from its inception as an innovative inevitability to its eventual end. Throughout his account, which is also a narrative experiment mixing criticism and fiction, he engaged with the historical and social aspects of the project as well as the technical aspects (Latour 1996b). In the early 1960s, the PRT systems seemed poised to dethrone the automobile as the future of transportation. This transportation system was supposed to combine the efficiency of an automated train with the convenience of personal transport. It implied walking into a car, entering your destination into a computer onboard, and walking out a few minutes later. A combination of private cars and public transportation that was to be accomplished by programming the individual cars to autonomously link up into trains when traveling in a group, and then splitting off onto branching paths as per the rider's destination. An innovative line of technology, mechanically inventive and politically relevant, it had so much promise.

Interviewing engineers, bureaucrats, and politicians in order to address the central question 'Who killed Aramis'? Latour investigated, like a detective, the failures in the socio-technical network that surrounded the concept of Aramis. The exploration of this question allowed him to bring his rhetorical resources to bear on his argument regarding the inclusion of nonhumans such as motors, chips, and PRT systems into his theoretical sociological network as actors in their own right. The concept of Aramis is enticing, but its execution proved to be rather complex.

As a prototype, Aramis was at the mercy of its makers – a diverse group, ranging from industrial kinematicians and satellite engineers to sympathetic bureaucrats and the Mayor of Paris. They could not agree on what Aramis was supposed to do and their views as to what killed Aramis ranged from fundamental technical failures to cynical political manoeuvring. After 50 interviews and a year of fieldwork, the author gathered not only one explanation but at least 20 different interpretations of the project that remain inseparable from the project itself.

> **To study Aramis, we also have to explain how certain points of view, certain perspectives, certain interpretations, have not had the means to impose themselves so as to become objects on which others have a simple point of view. So we have to pass from relativism to relationism. [...] The war of interpretations continues for Aramis; there are only perspectives, but these are not brought to bear on anything stable, since *no perspective has been able to stabilize the state of things to its own profit.***
>
> (Latour 1996b, 79; emphasis mine)

It is difficult to arrive at *the* interpretation, the correct explanation as to who or what killed Aramis. The sum of the interpretations of Aramis is hard to make, since there is no common intersection and hence no distinction between the interpretations and the object to be interpreted. Aramis remains a story, an argument, a quasi-object that circulates as a token in fewer and fewer hands. After 15 years, millions of francs, and the participation of dozens of governmental and private institutions, the project was abandoned as a failure.

The irony of the Aramis case is that the main engineers behind the project really believed in the epistemological (of how we can know the outside world) myth of a technology fully independent from society. Latour demonstrated that this is a pragmatic absurdity. To end the dualism of Society and Technology, and the partition between materialist and culturalist or sociological accounts, he engaged in a symmetrical anthropology of technology. In this enquiry, the object/objective substratum is no longer the unproblematic matter onto which cultures and societies add their view (Figure 4.3). When the attention shifts to the network of practices, the very notion of 'social meaning' fades away. Following this network and the trail of actors involved with Aramis, Latour concluded that Aramis was not deliberately 'killed'. There was no perpetrator, no guilty party. There was no Aramis affair, scandal, or public controversy. Rather, its trajectory 'depends not on the context but on the people who do the work of contextualizing' (Latour 1996b, 50). The individuals and the interest groups involved in its conception and creation failed to 'love' it, they stopped the negotiations, the research, and they abandoned it; or, in other words, they failed to engage with the concept of Aramis in a fashion that would make it a dynamic actor within the network of practice (Figure 4.3).

The case of Aramis demonstrates forcefully that the social construction of artefacts should be understood together with the technical construction of society. The idea that there are fixed human actors or fixed nonhuman actors that could be simply taken 'off the shelf' and inserted into the process is not helpful to understand its failure. As witnessed, the object is not positioned at one of the extremities while the social would be at the opposite (Figure 4.4). Instead, the body of the social element is constituted by machines (Latour 1993b). The

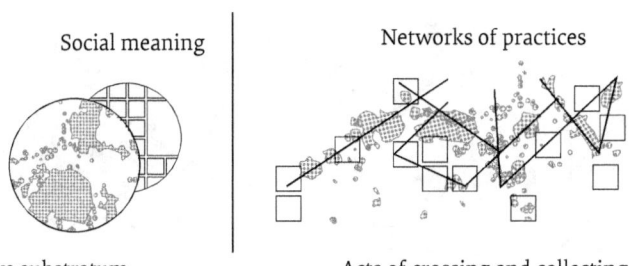

Figure 4.3 Networks of practices.
Illustration by Alexandra Arènes.

bureaucrats and the politicians do not know how they want to shape Aramis, and the software engineers do not know if they will be able to accommodate the contradictory wishes of different interest groups. As long as it exists, the technical object is the *institutionalised transaction* between humans and nonhumans through which elements of the actors' interests are reshaped and translated, while nonhuman competences are upgraded, shifted, folded or merged.

This process becomes accountable if we follow the translations of human and nonhuman competences instead of only following the displacements of the intentions of the human actors and their multiple interpretations. Therefore, the real locus of enquiry for the ethnographer of high technology is neither the technical object itself (the objective substratum), nor the social subjective interests (social meaning) (Figure 4.4). The locus of enquiry is to be found in the exchanges between the translated interests of humans and the delegated competences of nonhumans. As long as this exchange goes on, the project is alive and remains a possibility.

> the thing we are looking for is not a human thing, nor is it an inhuman thing. It offers, rather, a continuous passage, a commerce, an interchange, between what humans *inscribe* in it and what it *prescribes* to humans. It translates the one into the other. This thing is the nonhuman version of

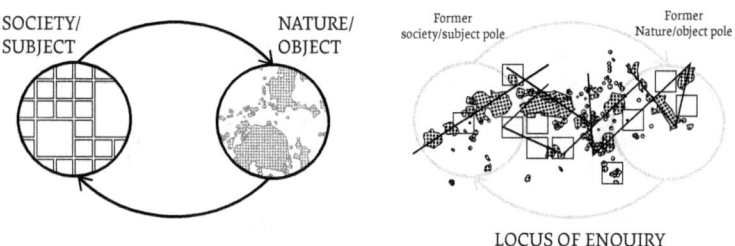

Figure 4.4 Locus of enquiry.
Illustration by Alexandra Arènes.

people, it is the human version of things, twice displaced. What should it be called? Neither object nor subject. An instituted object, quasi-object, quasi-subject, a thing that possesses body and soul indissolubly. The soul *of machines* constitutes the social element.

(Latour 1996b, 213)

The *thing*, the Aramis project, as we see, is a contested gathering of many conflicting demands; a disputed assemblage of humans and nonhumans. Paradoxically, many design objects often appear as *things* and not as mere objects; in design studies, new design artefacts are often a contested territory and their study cannot be reduced to a simple description of what they are materially, of how they function, and what they mean (Latour 2004a). As soon as a project is interrupted, or fails like Aramis, it dies, and we obtain, on the one hand, a social assembly of quarrelling human actors and, on the other, a stack of documents, and a pile of idle and rapidly decaying technical parts. As Latour stated, 'The distinction between objects and subjects is not primordial, it does not designate different domains in the world: it is rooted in the fracture of action' (Latour 1999a, 26). That fracture of action, that failure of the technical gesture, separates what is blended together in the repetitive act of making or in the use of the technological artefact. That is why in its normal functioning technology is an abstract system, often invisible; when it fails, it become visible, concrete, actual.

<u>As soon as a project is interrupted, or fails like Aramis, it dies, and we obtain, on the one hand, a social assembly of quarrelling human actors and, on the other, a stack of documents, and a pile of idle and rapidly decaying technical parts.</u>

Taking inspiration from Latour's anthropology of technology (both small mundane artefact and complex high-tech systems), it becomes important to study the work of success and failure in architectural design symmetrically. This would require scrutinising carefully the failed design projects (Yaneva 2009c), the unbuilt and highly controversial urban plans, the technological failure in urban contexts (Ross 2022; Simondon 1989; Shayya 2021). Both to study the work designers perform on the representation of users, but also, equally, the work they do on the representation of the design object itself (its agency, what it does, how it is perceived and apprehended). Scrutinising the object and the user, their relationship and the effects that the object generates on relevant social groups, is another way to introduce symmetrical thinking in design research.

CHAPTER 5

Actor-Network Theory

> It might be time to put Marx's famous quote back on its feet: 'Social scientists have transformed the world in various ways; the point, however, is *to interpret it*. But to interpret, we need to abandon the strange idea that all languages are translatable in the already established idiom of the social.
>
> (Latour 2005b, 42; emphasis mine)

In light of the sociology of science and technology of Latour it is difficult to accept a traditional definition of society. Latour, in collaboration with anthropologist Shirley Strum, distinguished two types of social link (Strum and Latour 1987). *First*, the ostensive definition. According to this traditional way of thinking, society exists and actors enter it adhering to rules and a structure that are already determined. The overall nature of the society is unknown and unknowable to the actors who blindly take part in it. Only those standing outside of society – the sociologists – have the capacity to understand it and see it in its entirety. *Second*, the performative definition. According to the performative view, society is constructed through the many efforts to define it. It is something achieved in practice by all actors involved, including sociologists, who strive to define what society is. An example is the society of baboons observed by Strum: constantly testing, trying to see who is allied with whom, who is leading whom, and so on – both baboons and scientists end up asking the same questions. As baboons are constantly negotiating, *the social link* is transformed into a process of acquiring knowledge about 'what the society is'. Endorsing a performative view, Strum and Latour argued that society is continually constructed or 'performed' by active social beings who disrupt both micro and macro 'levels' in the process of their activities, their 'work'.

<u>According to the performative view, society is constructed through the many efforts to define it. It is something achieved in practice by all actors involved.</u>

Society or the making of the social

Latour reflected extensively on the questions of society and the methods to study social links in his acclaimed book *Reassembling the Social* (2005b), where he set out the methodological principles of Actor-Network Theory (ANT). He asked: 'What is a society? What does the word "social" mean? Why are some activities said to have a "social dimension"? How can one demonstrate the presence of "social factors" at work?' (Latour 2005b, 3). Society is often understood as the 'hidden source of causality' that accounts for the existence and stability of different types of action or behaviour. There is an implicit role given to the social sciences when explanation is at stake: they are expected to provide the solutions. It is assumed that the social should provide the explanation and occupy the position of a cause. Other realms (science, technology, markets, but also the built environment and infrastructure) are treated as the phenomena that are to be explained and are often considered as effects of social causes. Yet, Latour demonstrated that the social sciences are part and parcel of the activities that we want to study; they are part of our problem, not the solution to the problem and they will not lead us to a better understanding of these realities (Latour 1988b). Causality in the social sciences needs to be entirely rethought. Engaging in a critique of all attempts of social explanation, Latour argued that no explanation has ever consisted of anything more than a disproportionate amount of heterogeneous, historical, and contingent elements. There is an inherent contradiction in trying to explain different phenomena with the resources of the social sciences. In other words, the 'social' is not that which should *explain*, but that which requires an explanation through empirical investigation.

Therefore, Latour argued against the habit of linking the notions of 'society', 'social factor', 'power', 'structure' and 'context' with vast arrays of life and history in order to reveal, behind the scenes, some dark powers pulling the strings. He claimed that instead of doing these jumps from 'society' to an empirical reality, that 'the time has come to have a much closer look at the type of aggregates thus assembled and at the ways they are connected to one another' (Latour 2005b, 22), that is, to engage in tracing the composition of the social. Instead of a homogenous substance, the social is a way of connecting heterogeneous actors and environments; it is to be composed, made up, constructed, established, maintained, and assembled. It is far from being a synonym of society.

This understanding of the social is at the heart of Actor-Network Theory (ANT). An ANT enquiry begins with a number of controversies around different types of uncertainties.

First, there are uncertainties surrounding the nature of groups: one can belong to many different groups at the same time and can gain an identity in different ways. From an ANT perspective it is important not to settle on one privileged grouping, but to acknowledge that there are lots of contradictory group formations, and processes of enrolment into groups. In addition, there is no privileged language to study groups, but ANT prefers to use what could be called an *infra-language*; this is a way for the vocabulary of the actors to be heard loud and clear instead of translating this language into the jargon of social scientists. Social aggregates are then not the object of an ostensive definition – like mugs, cats, and chairs that can be pointed at by an index finger – but only of a performative definition – of following the actors as they relate to one another, as groups take form, and also in terms of how they understand themselves and their relations with others.

Second, there is uncertainty around the nature of actions: in each course of action a great variety of agents seem to intervene and displace the original goals. This type of uncertainty deals with the heterogeneous nature of the ingredients making up social ties. Latour asked: 'When we act, who else is acting? How many agents are also present? How come I never do what I want? Why are we all held by forces that are not of our own making?' (Latour 2005b, 43). Action does not take a simple route, but is overtaken, taken up by others, and shared with the masses. It is mysteriously carried out and at the same time distributed to others. We are not alone in the world. Avoiding all determinations, Latour emphasised the under-determination of action, the uncertainties and controversies about who and what is acting when 'we' act. This source of uncertainty can reside in the analyst or in the actor. The actor is never alone in acting, but is rather part of a thick imbroglio where the question of *who* or *what* is carrying out the action is indeterminate. Like an actor in a theatre play, she needs support personnel, lighting, scripts, a backstage crew, reactions from the audience, partners, etc. Unfolding the play-acting metaphor, Latour outlined the way the term 'actor' directs our attention to a *complete dislocation of the action*, warning us that it is not a coherent, controlled, well-rounded, and clean-edged affair. Action is dislocated. 'An "actor" in the hyphenated expression actor-network is not the source of an action but the moving target of a vast array of entities swarming toward it' (Latour 2005b, 56). If action is dislocated, it does not pertain to any specific site; it is distributed, variegated, multiple, and remains a puzzle for the analysts as well as for the actors. To understand the nature of action and how it is distributed, ANT researchers should 'follow the actors themselves'.

Latour outlined the way the term 'actor' directs our attention to a *complete dislocation of the action*, warning us that it is not a coherent, controlled, well-rounded, and clean-edged affair.

Third, there is uncertainty around the nature of objects: the type of agencies participating in an interaction themselves are indeterminate. For ANT, the definition of the term social does not designate a domain of reality, but rather points to a movement, a displacement, a transformation, a translation, an enrolment, and an association between entities which are in no way recognisable as being social (e.g. the microbes of Pasteur or the Berlin Key).

If we follow the actors in their weaving through things, what renders the constantly shifting interactions more durable are the objects, numerous objects. ANT considers objects as *potential* participants in the course of actions. Thus, starting from the controversies about actors and agencies, anything that makes a difference is an actor, and there is a trail that allows someone to detect this difference. Objects are actors as they leave traces behind and they modify states of affairs; they make a difference.

However, it would be wrong to assume that objects determine action; they simply allow, afford, encourage, authorise, suggest, influence, block, render possible, forbid, and so on. In other words, there are many metaphysical shades between full causality and sheer inexistence. ANT is not the empty claim that objects do things 'instead' of humans. It invites us to thoroughly explore the question of *who and what participates in the action* without privileging humans or nonhumans in advance. Latour wrote:

> once you realize that any human course of action might weave together in a matter of minutes, for instance, a shouted order to lay a brick, the chemical connection of cement with water, the force of a pulley unto a rope with a movement of the hand, the strike of a match to light a cigarette offered by a co-worker, etc. Here, the apparently reasonable division between material and social becomes just what is obfuscating any enquiry on how a collective action is possible.
>
> (Latour 2005b, 74)

In the vertigo of action it is impossible to separate material and social entities. We witness an action that is not carried over by homogeneous social forces, but, on the contrary, 'an action that collects different types of forces woven together because they are different' (Latour 2005b, 86). This is how a *collective* is shaped. A collective also designates the process of assembling new entities not yet gathered together and which are not made of social stuff. In the course of an action, a symmetry is established between these entities, that is, to not assume a false asymmetry between human action and a material world of causal relations. The division between powerful humans and a passive objective world is one that we should never try to bypass or overcome, argued Latour, but rather ignore.

Objects, by the very nature of their connections with humans, quickly shift from being mediators (that translate and modify meaning) to intermediaries (that transport meaning without transformation). This is why specific tricks have to be invented to make them talk, that is, to offer descriptions of themselves and to account for what they make us do. Where can we see this happening? We can study innovations in the artisan's workshop, the engineer's design department, the scientist's laboratory, the marketer's trial panels, the user's home, and the many different controversies that unfold at these places. On these sites, objects live a complex life through meetings, plans, sketches, regulations, and trials. There, objects can be maintained longer as visible mediators actively translating and transforming meaning – due to their uncertainty – before becoming invisible, asocial intermediaries. That is where agencies are made to express themselves. Another way: when users approach objects and technologies, their ignorance and clumsiness can also render objects visible as mediators. Accidents, breakdowns, and strikes can offer other occasions to witness the role of mediators, where, suddenly, completely silent intermediaries become full blown mediators, forcing actors to re-group and re-assemble to *deal* with them. Objects can also be brought back from archives. Documents, memoirs, museum collections, can be made to act as mediators through historians' and archivists' accounts (Mitchell 2022). My study of architectural archiving, based on ethnography at the Canadian Centre for Architecture (CCA) in Montreal and the archive of Álvaro Siza in Portugal, demonstrated how in the process of collecting, processing and conserving architectural objects, archival materials become active mediators in the crafting of knowledge of importance to the discipline of architecture (Yaneva 2020). Finally, the resources of fiction can turn the solid objects of today into fluid entities where their connections with humans may make sense. These are possible empirical sites of research that ANT invites us to explore in order to renew empiricism.

Fourth, there is uncertainty around the nature of facts: the links of natural sciences with the rest of society are sources of continuous disputes. Latour clarified that 'constructivism' should not be confused with 'social constructivism'. For a fact to be constructed, simply means to account for its solid objective reality which is the result of the mobilisation of various entities and its eventual stabilisation. 'Social constructivism' means, on the other hand, that we replace what this reality is made of with some other stuff, the social in which it is 'really' built. Yet, for any construction to take place, nonhuman entities play a major role. Referring to his ethnography of scientific practices, Latour claimed that 'objects of science may explain the social, not the other way around. No experience was more striking than what I saw with my own eyes: the social explanation had vanished into thin air' (Latour 2005b, 99). One week in the laboratory of Roger Guillemin was enough for him to conclude that the social cannot be substituted for the smallest rock, the tiniest polypeptide, the most innocuous electron, the tamest baboon. That is why compositionism is a better term than constructivism (Latour 2010b).

For ANT scholars, to explain is to engage in a practical world-building enterprise that consists in connecting entities with other entities, that is, in tracing a network, rather than engaging in social explanations and comparing cause with effect(s). For instance, in the classic ANT example of Michel Callon (1986a), fishermen, oceanographers, satellites, and scallops form relations with one another, relations of such a sort that they make others do unexpected things. An ANT account traces their connections and shows how they do things to one another, and become mediators for each other. 'The social is nowhere in particular as a thing among other things but may circulate everywhere as a movement connecting non-social things' (Latour 2005b, 107). In ANT terms, the British Empire, for instance, is not 'behind' Lord Kelvin's telegraph experiments in order to explain them. In 1858, Kelvin's team invented an instrument called a 'mirror galvanometer', which measures the electric current flowing through the cable. After a number of failures and lost signals, they eventually succeeded in installing the first trans-Atlantic telegraph in 1866. This made it possible to connect distant parts of the empire and strengthened its economic power. British expertise in cable-engineering was recognised internationally and Kelvin's techniques and instruments were used for cables in various parts of the world. Thus, we can argue that the British Empire gained a reach and a durability thanks to the tiny cables laid out on the ocean that linked its far-flung locations. Kelvin's science creates, in part, the Empire, which is no longer in the background but is made to exist through telegraph wires. The cables, in other words, operate as mediators. It is this reversal in causality that ANT tries to register.

> I can now state the aim of this sociology of associations more precisely: there is no society, no social realm, and no social ties, but there exist translations between mediators that may generate traceable associations.
> (Latour 2005b, 108)

<u>For ANT scholars, to explain is to engage in a practical world-building enterprise that consists in connecting entities with other entities, that is, in tracing a network, rather than engaging in social explanations and comparing cause with effect(s).</u>

Tracing associations, we witness a shift from the world of matters of fact to the worlds of *matters of concern*, highly uncertain and disputed agencies, taken as gatherings, as associations, and not as self-sufficient objects. Engaging in exploring and mapping scientific controversies about matters of concern, ANT renders untenable the divide between one unified reality, intact and remote, and many possible subjective interpretations or social explanations of it.

Lastly, the *fifth* uncertainty is about the type of studies done under the label of a science of the social as it is never clear in which precise sense social sciences can be said to be empirical. The solution to relativism, for Latour, is always more *relativity*. Therefore, ANT written accounts should foreground *the relations* and *the tracing of the social*, its process of reassembling, reiterated Latour. 'I would define a good account as one that traces a network' (Latour 2005b, 128). Thus, a good ANT description offers a narrative where all the actors do something; instead of transporting effects without transforming them, 'each of the points in the text may become a bifurcation, an event, or the origin of a new translation' (Latour 2005b, 128). This will require treating actors as mediators (not intermediaries) and rendering the movement of the social visible to the reader in a way that the network will showcase the ability of each actor to make other actors do unexpected things. The task of ANT accounts is to deploy (not just describe or reveal the social forces behind) actors as networks of mediations – hence the hyphen in the composite word 'actor-network'. By doing so, a good account does not simply narrate the social, it performs the social in the precise sense that some of the participants in the action will be assembled and collected together.

These five uncertainties help to reveal: What is the social made up of? What is acting when we are acting? What sort of grouping do we pertain to? What do we want? What sort of world are we ready to share? All those questions are raised not only by scholars, but also by the actors themselves.

Yet, if we trace how fisherman and scallops, Kelvin and cables relate to one another, how do we go from local interactions to global entities and meaning? How do we move from the *micro* to the *macro*? The global, Latour argued, is to be relocated so as to break down the automatism that leads from interaction to 'context', from the micro to the marco (Figure 5.1). The latter, for instance, no longer describes a wider or a larger site in which the former would be embedded, but another equally local, equally 'micro' place, which is connected to many others. 'What is now highlighted much more vividly than before are all the connections, the cables, the means of transportation, the vehicles linking places together. This is their strength but also, as we are going to see, their frailty' (Latour 2005b, 176). Thus, the macro is neither 'above' nor 'below' the interactions but *added* to them as another connection. It is when we replace actors of whatever size by local and connected sites, instead of ranking them into micro and macro categories, that we witness actor-networks. But not only is the global an abstraction that has to be *localised*, but face-to-face interaction

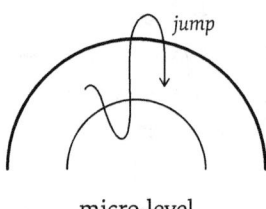

Figure 5.1 Plasma.
Illustration by Alexandra Arènes.

is also an abstraction that has to be re-dispatched and redistributed. The sites revealed, as a result, are to be connected; there is a *flattening* of the social, which highlights the definition of the social as associations.

For Latour, the social world occupies a very different position from the one that traditional social scientists attribute to it. It is not behind the scenes, above our heads, or before the action, but *after the action, below the participants, and smack in the middle of the foreground*. It neither encompasses nor explains; it circulates, coordinates, and requires explanation. In fact, the social world explored so far is the equivalent of the London tube network on the map of London. There is a vast territory that is not yet formatted, measured, socialised, engaged in metrological chains, and covered over. This is what Latour called *plasma* (Figure 5.1): 'The plasma would be the rest of London, all its buildings, inhabitants, climates, plants, cats, palaces, horse guards' (Latour 2005b, 244). ANT invites us to explore this uncharted territory, the plasma.

An ANT approach to architecture

Translating the pitfalls of social explanations in architecture would mean questioning the assumption that casts social factors as the cause, where architecture is reduced to the effect. We tend to explain the development of buildings and urban form by magically invoking a social force like the mazes of bureaucracy, the disruptions of political disagreements and the constraints of economic relations. A flurry of studies in architecture since the 1980s have attempted to discern *the exact relationship between architecture and society*, claiming that the key to understanding the built environments lays with a comprehension of the society and culture in which they exist (King 1980) or advocating a role of architecture as pattern giver to society (Evans 1982). Yet, following Latour, we should remind ourselves that architecture uses a reservoir of notions that do not always translate easily into social terms. Not all aspects of architectural technology, materiality and tectonics can be reduced to social dimensions. Moreover, substituting the built form with social dimensions does not lead us to a better understanding of architecture. ANT invites us to reconsider the regime of causation in studies of architecture. If Society does not have a stable reservoir of meanings to explain architecture, what is left to be explained is – 'everything' – both society and architecture, social factors and built form. Rethinking causation will lead us to the *first advantage of an ANT perspective to architecture*: instead of evaluating the impact of external factors/context on design/content, architecture can be grasped *in concreto*.

Following Latour, we should remind ourselves that architecture uses a reservoir of notions that do not always translate easily into social terms.

An ANT approach in the field of architectural history and theory will inspire tracing and carefully accounting for urban and design realities (Cronon 1991; Doucet 2015; Zitouni 2010), rather than quickly explaining them. Follow the long, contingent and painstaking process of making a building, the process of dwelling or urban contestation, and not the building ready-made; allow yourself the time to explore its multifarious features as they unfold in design trials, or in the experiences of inhabitation, all the mediators and all the connections traced, and you will find out that there are not two separate worlds: a possible behind the real, a symbolic realm behind the objective, or a society behind architecture. There is no built content on one side, and, at a cosmic distance, a social context, on the other. We rather witness how a design project can modify the elements that contextualise it, triggering contextual mutations. In this sense, it resembles more a complex ecology than it does a static object (Latour and Yaneva 2008). Context is variable, moving, evolving and changing along with the various design objects themselves; context is made of the many dimensions that impinge at every stage on the development of a project. In the heat of the action, everything is fluid, all artificial divides are redistributed, all static categories collapse, and all we witness is a socio-architectural assemblage made out of heterogeneous stuff: models, architects, zoning regulations, mayors, public money, techniques of calculating construction budgets, heritage organisations, and a vast array of materials. An ANT study of architecture allows us to gain access to that particular moment when the divide between content and context has not been made yet. A moment when the architectural and the social are fluid and mutually define each other – a unique instant when all redistributions are possible.

Expanding the project of ANT to the field of architecture requires mobilising Latour's persistent ambition to account for and understand (not replace) objects, institutions and cultures. This is *a second advantage of ANT*. We should not limit our analysis to the discourses of designers and inventors. Tackling their stories of invention falsely separates the aesthetic and the technical, form and function, styling and engineering. It prevents us from embracing the diversity of the creative process. An ANT approach consists in scrutinising the practices of designing architects rather than their big theories and ideologies; it prioritises the pragmatic content of actions, not of discourses. Tracing *architecture in the making* (Armando and Durbiano 2017; Houdart and Minato 2009; Mommersteeg 2020; Yaneva 2005, 2009a; Yarrow 2019) we follow the design routines, the mistakes, the mundane technical and material choices of architects and many other participants in design, we account for their actions and transactions in complex spatial settings. It is here that mediators multiply. We witness the materialisation of successive operations on a daily basis, as well as their, sometimes, surprising and unforeseen effects. Capturing the movements of designers in the studio, how they handle models, sketches, software, how they attribute meaning to their actions, how they negotiate and form different groupings, will lead us to understand design as a process of enacting the social. In this process, there are no single actors, mastering and controlling creation:

> There is no control and no all-powerful creator, either – no more 'God' than man – but there is care, scruple, cautiousness, attention, contemplation, hesitation and revival. To understand each other, all we have is what comes from our own hands, but that doesn't mean our hands can be taken for the origin.
>
> (Latour 2013, 144)

Tracing architecture in the making with care, caution and respect to all participants, we witness buildings that are not made by powerful minds (star architects, demiurges, those powerful 'Gods'), but architecture that emerges as it traces many intricate and hesitant relationships with materials and technologies, skills, bodies and institutions.

A third advantage of an ANT approach to architecture is that it does justice to the many material dimensions of things without limiting them in advance to pure material properties or to social symbols. It offers an ample view of the multidimensional, active and surprising nature of things. Design, thus, embraces a complex conglomerate of many surprising agencies. To understand the activities of humans, their passions, we need to also turn our attention to what makes them active, to their attachments, and their concerns.

<u>To understand the activities of humans, their passions, we need to also turn our attention to what makes them active, to their attachments, and their concerns.</u>

An ANT perspective thus implies unpacking the *attachments* of designers to things in the creative process. Contrary to what we are used to believing as 'moderns', attachments do not immobilise action, restrict a 'will' or paralyse the world, it is rather the attachments that put it in motion, that provide the power to act. To illustrate the power of attachments, Latour brought examples from music, writing and addiction. Does a smoker smoke? Or, does the cigarette smoke him? Is a writer in control of writing, or is it the writing that is writing her? You believe you love Bach, and you play the piano, but the piano is playing you, you are *overtaken* by the music (Gomart and Hennion 1999). You think you speak English, but that language is speaking you (right now!). These attachments are revealing for understanding what things make us do, or to use the French term, *faire-faire* (to make one do something). Is a smoker capable of controlling his action where the cigarette is simply smoked (he acts, and the cigarette does nothing), or is he completely controlled by the object, the cigarette, the addiction (the cigarette acts, he does nothing)? What stands in the middle between these traditional positions, of freedom and determinism, is the *factish* (Latour 2010c). Latour constructed this term with the words of 'fact' and 'fetish', where fact refers to the positivist discourse of verification and fetish to the critical discourse of denunciation. The factish underlines the work of fabrication and points to *what* makes us do things, to what makes us act. It takes the attention away from the obsessive distinction between the rational (facts) and the irrational (fetishes) and the obsession for *locating* the cause of an action.

How often does the work of designers also stand between freedom and determinations? If we follow design in the making, a sociology of factishes, of mediations, will better reveal its inner working dynamics. Models, software, sketches, and programming all make designers act, think and create in a specific way. It is neither the model nor the designer but that very specific attachment between them that acts in a design process. Architects remain constantly attached to these beings, and the proliferation of visual tools in design creates more sources of attachment. In the heart of design action, we are no longer thinking of what acts and what is made, what is active and what is passive. In the process of design, we are (just like writers, musicians, and smokers) positioned to pursue a chain of mediators. We are no more in control of what we make or design than we are subjects to control; we are attached to models and sketches, codes and software. There is no *escape* from these attachments, no absolute emancipation. There are only other attachments, substitutes. During my ethnography of the practice of OMA (Yaneva 2005, 2009b, 2009c), for instance, Rem Koolhaas realised that the attachment to blue foam in the office was excessive and introduced an experiment: 'one month without blue foam'; after prolonged discussions on how to respond to this provocation, designers suggested replacing the blue foam with white foam, or to move from one form of attachment to another; yet, a complete detachment from foam was impossible. Thus, I experienced, first-hand, the impossibility of designers to move from a state of attachment to that of unattachment. To better understand the world of design and of architects, their passions, their emotions, their driving forces, we need to turn attention to that which attaches and activates them.

We are no more in control of what we make or design than we are subjects to control; we are attached to models and sketches, codes and software.

We all have multiple attachments, argued Latour, and we often substitute one attachment with another, but the attribution of a clear source of action is not possible (it is neither me, nor my sketch!). As Latour wrote, 'As powerful as one might imagine a creator, he will never be capable of better controlling his creations than the puppeteer her puppets, a writer his notebooks, a cigarette its smoker, a speaker her language. He can make them do something, but he cannot *make* them' (Latour 1999a, 28). We are never the masters of our tools, of our creations.

> Who has ever seen a builder actually master his building? Where is the creator who feels himself capable of controlling his creature? What

> robotician thinks he's the master of his robots, what marionettist isn't taught amazing tricks by his marionettes?
>
> (Latour 2013, 143)

As creators we are always surprised by events that we cannot control, but that we make happen, which are consequences. Just as a robotician cannot fully master a robot, architects are unable to master their buildings, we cannot *make* them fully, but we can 'make them do something'. Moreover, it is time to rethink, Latour argued, the old opposition between attachment and detachment (we hardly move from one state of attachment towards a state of detachment as shown through the blue foam story at OMA). We should rather replace this opposition with good and bad attachments, attachments that kill and attachments that save, attachments that increase the power to act and attachments that decrease the power to act. Placed between the two extremities of necessity/determination/structure and freedom/freewill/subjectivity are a large number of attachments to different types of beings. These are precisely the attachments that make us exist. Substituting one type of attachment with another, moving from one type of entanglement to an even bigger entanglement, from modern to non-modern (rather than moving from the state of non-modern to modern), we find ourselves in a *network of attachments*. This allows us to maintain the distributive effects of the network and enables us to re-conceptualise the nature and the source of creative action. Architectural networks of attachments, however, are yet to be fully explored.

CHAPTER 6

Space and spacing

'It's sunny, this morning on the Neuchâtel lake, and windy and cold. What's that bright little shape out there?' (Latour 1997, 173). That is how Latour began a seminal essay on the fabrication of space and time. It turns out that the bright little shape out there is a surfboarder moving fast in the wind. Getting close to the observer sitting at the edge of the water, the face of the surfboarder becomes visible. He seems to enjoy himself; he does not see *time passing by*. Is he moving like an arrow in 'lived' time and space? Unlikely. 'Lived', Latour argued, is one of these empty words. Often, lived time and lived space is set in opposition to the more 'accurate' definition of a timeless and space-less instant and place. An opposition between the richness of a *lived* experience of time and space and the empty Cartesian grid. Yet, Latour claimed that following the moves of the surfboarder there is no point in opposing and comparing lived time to real time, or subjective experience to objective experience. The calculation of speed and the apparatus to extract speed from the surfboarder are *both inside* the world where he sails fast. Objective experience is not the 'depth' feature on which his own psychological world or subjective experience would be built. The 'lived' is not just a false decorative layer coated upon a bleak reality made of measurements. Watch the surfboarder: he is grinning, moving quickly towards the beach, turning unpredictably, bending swiftly, enjoying himself, guided by the waves. His brisk veers, the movements of the wind, and the sides of the lake you notice while watching him all paint a picture of his experience. Getting closer to this experience, Latour wrote,

> Enjoyment. That is the space-time in which he resides and moves. He is no more moving in space than he is in time. He is not adding a subjective morning to real mornings. Subjective lakes to real lakes. He explores *the multiplicity of ways of being*, he goes from some to many, from boring to alert ones, from a little wind to a fierce gale, from a low intensity to a higher intensity. Yes, that's it, he is moving into enjoyment, intensity,

ways of being, alterations, and if I want to calculate his speed, I can, but I won't define the depth of his world, the backdrop of all existence.

(Latour 1997, 174)

In other words, there is no need either to turn back to the objective calculation of time or towards the psychologically colourful lived experience. To find richness, we should simply 'turn towards the world itself', to the wind, the foam, the sun, the snow-capped mountains in the back of the Swiss lake, the earnest miniature city behind the harbour, the glowing face of the surfboarder. This would mean to immerse ourselves *in the process of surfing*, where we are neither just in time nor just in space. 'Process is a third term, as if the surfboarder were moving into ways of being, exploring its alterity, its alterations' (Latour 1997, 174). Following processes, we escape landing on both the solid shores of objective or subjective interpretations. This would mean to explore fully all mediations in practice (as a surfboarder moves or a designer creates) without falling into the trap of subjective or objective explanations.

<u>Following processes, we escape landing on both the solid shores of objective or subjective interpretations. This would mean to explore fully all mediations in practice.</u>

Process and the construction of space

To develop this understanding of process further, as it opens a third avenue between subjective and objective time, let us follow two siblings travelling – not in water this time, but on the ground! – to unravel what Latour coined as 'the paradox of the twin travellers'. Imagine two twins. The first sets off in a deep jungle and cuts her way with a hatchet along a trail which is barely visible. Each minute that she travels, she ages more than one minute. She sweats. Her body bears the traces of her efforts; each metre can be read in the bloody scars made by thorns and ferns. We witness her struggle, and her suffering, surrounded by other suffering bodies, vines, grass, and trees. She remembers every bit of this excruciating experience as each stretch of the trip is traversed and won over through a complicated 'negotiation' with other entities, the mud, humidity, branches, wild animals that she comes across.

In comparison with this struggling twin, her twin brother sits comfortably in a train. Sat quietly in his air-conditioned carriage, relaxing, listening to music, reading a newspaper, paying no attention to the number of places crossed by the speeding train, this twin remains ignorant of the jungle struggles of his sister. He does not age more than the two hours of the trip. His body does not bear any trace of the voyage. He will have no recollection of this trip except having boarded the train. The travel remains invisible, unmemorable as no negotiations with strange creatures – mud, animals and uneven terrain – were needed along the way. An *uneventful* trip, nothing to mention.

Comparing these two twins and the way they age, Latour directed our attention to the mechanics of fabrication of times and, in particular, the relation between *transportation* and *transformation*. If the woman traveller is modified and ages more than a bit, the male traveller is not modified by the trip at all. Thus, the first traveller will equate transportation (or displacement) with modification, aging, history, transformation, metamorphosis. For the second one, in contrast, there will be two apparently different phenomena: moving through space in time, on the one hand, and aging, living, suffering, and participating in events, on the other hand. Immersed in the process of travelling, the jungle voyager does not differentiate space, time, and aging, whereas her twin brother distinguishes what is displaced from the immutable framework in which it is displaced. It is the relation between transportation and transformation that differs in both cases, and therefore, *the production of times and spaces* will be entirely different.

Situating his understanding of times and spaces within the Leibnizian tradition, Latour stated that instead of the classic opposition between time and space, we witness, as we follow the processual trajectory of the jungle traveller – just like we followed the surfboarder on that sunny morning on the Neuchâtel lake or designers and engineers at work trying to solve the glare problem in Birmingham – a varying range of entities, beings and events. Thus, both time and space appear as consequences of the ways in which bodies relate to one another. Space and time are not abstractions; they rather *express some specific relation between the entities themselves*. We can generate as many spaces and times as there are types of relations. The difference between the two voyagers comes from the number of others one has to take into account, and their nature (if they are passive, docile *intermediaries* or active *mediators*). Timing depends on that sort of ontological difference, not on the mind's apperception; the more entities we need for our existence, the more time and space will proliferate. The speed of the train and the uneventful trip of the passenger are entirely dependent on the complete obedience of the places that are traversed and also, of course, on the smooth functioning of the train companies, organisation, engineers, the rail network, etc. If all of them work, if the train does not breakdown, if the railway line is maintained, if a crowd of protesters do not block its way, they remain invisible; this is another important dimension to take into account (in addition to the relation between *transportation* and *transformation*) when tackling space and time construction: *the relative visibility of the work to be done in order to obtain a displacement*.

<u>Both time and space appear as consequences of the ways in which bodies relate to one another. Space and time are not abstractions; they rather *express some specific relation between the entities themselves.*</u>

Spacing

Our civilisation has long had a fixation on how best to transport something without de-forming it, to generate constants that can be carried around and that resist deformation in spite of transportation, what Latour has called *immutable mobiles* (Latour 1987). In a world made of intermediaries, of displacement without transformation, there is a time separated from space, an immutable frame to measure displacements and, by definition, no process. In a world made of mediations, of transportation by deformation, there are a lot of times and places (as experienced by the jungle traveller engaged in trail-making). Thus, Latour argued powerfully,

> **we should not speak of time, space, and actant but rather of temporalization, spatialization, actantialization (the words are horrible) or more elegantly, of timing, spacing, acting.**
>
> (Latour 1997, 178)

Moreover, the question of spacing, timing and acting should always be combined with that of their intensity (Figure 6.1). An intensity we often experience as designers in our attempts to factor in the nature and the various activities of those who will participate in spacing. It is the intensity of time and space that defines their deeper definition, depending on the otherness, on the quality of connection with other actants. This is what Latour identified as the fifth dimension of time: *process*. The intensity of time is defined as opposite to its expansion.

As process is equally connected to time and space, Latour launched an appeal to 'elevate spacing to the same philosophical dignity as timing' (Latour 1997, 180) and outlined the labour that goes into the fabrication of spaces and times. Thus, space is not a passive framework 'out there', a container that can be filled in with activities (and we can say also with buildings and infrastructures) but is rather generated by work. Therefore, there will be no buildings *in* space since times and spaces are generated by a certain type of work and the displacement of certain kinds of bodies that usually remain invisible. There are a number of techniques that provide peculiar ways of folding times and actants of different qualities and tempos (Latour 1994, 1996a). Far from being a point in space, a site met by the traveller who comes back becomes a connection of interactions dispersed in

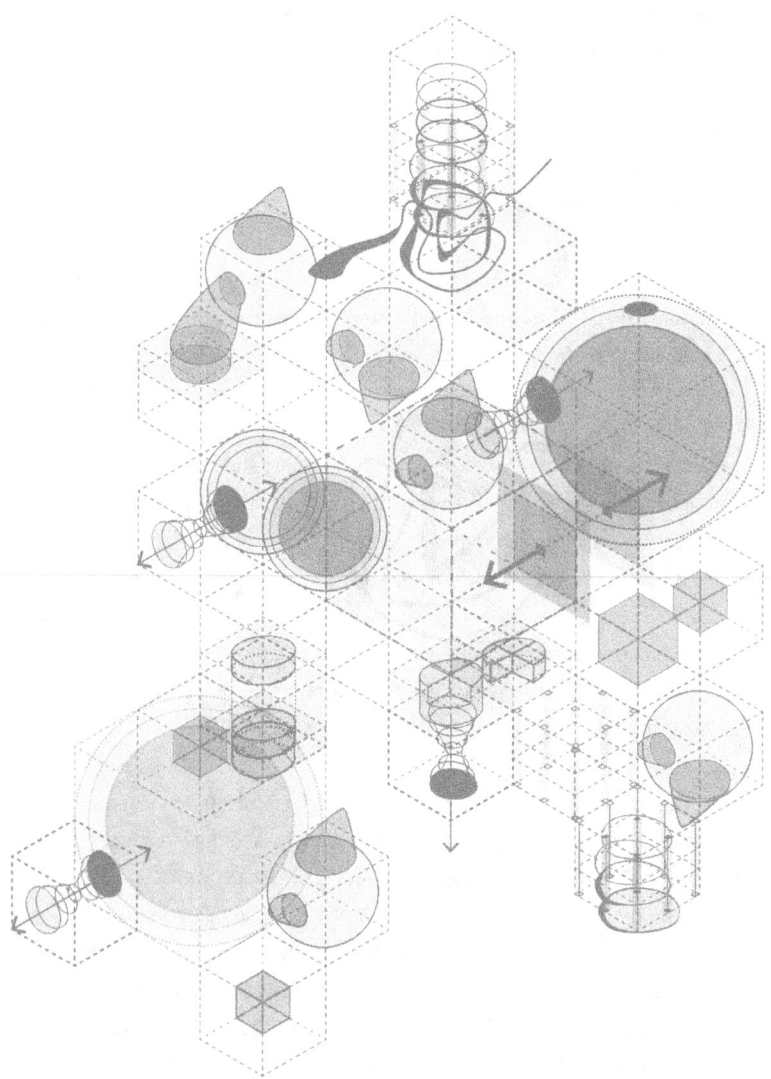

Figure 6.1 Spacing.
Illustration by Alexandra Arènes.

time, space, and action and reassembled again in a place. Thus, a building we might argue, following this way of thinking, occupies space, creates a landscape, becomes a landmark, etc, not because it is a spot *in* space, but because it is itself the event connecting multiple interactions on a large spread of space-time actants. Conceptualising buildings not as simple obedient objects we design and insert into an empty space, but rather as events, will require a total rethinking of both architectural practice and users' experience.

<u>A building we might argue, following this way of thinking, occupies space, creates a landscape, becomes a landmark, etc, not because it is a spot *in* space, but because it is itself the event connecting multiple interactions on a large spread of space-time actants.</u>

If we follow architects at work in a design studio or the multifarious ways of inhabiting a building (Hansmann 2021), we never encounter time and space, but a multiplicity of interactions with actants having their own timing, spacing, goals, means, and ends. We witness that there is no single time and single space, but designers at work rely on the subversion, disjunction, displacement, rescaling, and crossing-over of relations between spatial, actorial, and temporal features. If we follow users in a building, the one time-and-space formula swiftly becomes an abstraction. Long before we talk of space and time, there are all sorts of connections, short-circuits, translations, associations, and mediations that we encounter daily. That is why it is not useful to oppose the 'lived world' of human subjectivity (of both designers and users) apprehending space and time, intentions, and affectivity to the scientific and technical objective world 'ceaselessly beating the isotopic and isochronic meaningless space-time' (Latour 1997, 182).

In *Irreductions* (1.2.6) written as a philosophical appendix to *The Pasteurization of France* (1988a), Latour wrote:

> **Space and time do not frame entelechies [actualities]. They only become frameworks of description for those actants that have submitted, locally and provisionally, to the hegemony [domination] of another. There is therefore a time of times and a space of spaces, and so on until everything has been negotiated.**
>
> (Latour 1988a, 165)

Thus, one thing cannot be reduced to another, one actor to another; reduction is not productive because it shows *less* of the world or of experience. If we believe that one actor may contain the others, we start to believe that we 'know' something, that there are equivalences, that there are simple deductions, that there is some order in advance. Latour adopted the opposite principle, of irreduction, that claims that nothing can be reduced to anything else. Things are linked together *symmetrically*; they form knots, bodies, machines, and groups. Since there are no 'natural' equivalences, the kind of ties that hold things together can only be of one kind: groping, testing, translating. When we accept the principle of irreducibility, we admit that there is nothing more than trials of strength and weakness, work to be done, gestures.

> **If we choose the principle of *reduction, it gives us plain, clean surfaces*. But since there are many surfaces, they have to be ordered, and since they each occupy the whole of space, then they fight one another. It is necessary to survey their boundaries. (...) If we choose the principle of irreduction, *we discover intertwined networks* which sometimes join together but may interweave with each other without touching for centuries. (...) There is no more totality, so nothing is left over. It seems to me that life is better this way.**
>
> (Latour 1988a, 190–191)

Latour's philosophy invites us to trace the *intertwined networks of practice*, like those in the practices of architectural design and planning in which space is actively dissected and observed, folded and unfolded, as reports and technologies, measurements and tests circulate. Space appears as more than a container, an object or a social construct. Following Latour, we can trace design and construction processes, as sets of movements sculpting networks, of processes that create various kinds of spaces and times. How often do we encounter a site, a place, a space that is simply 'out there': physical, static, and passively awaiting the intervention of an adventurous designer? Conversely, how often is a site a pure social construction: a cultural product that is fabricated alongside another cultural constructions, a building or type of infrastructure? Latour helps us move beyond the stubbornness of a site *as* plane surface, and against the relativity of a site *as* social construct, not by adding them as two absolutes, but by focusing on what is frequently forgotten: how site/space *matters* in design, planning and construction processes and the work that is needed to fabricate spaces and times, the spacing and timing of the world. More studies are needed to unpack specific situations where the work of spacing, timing, placing and siting becomes visible (Yaneva and Mommersteeg 2019). Tracing these moves will allow a better understanding of the malleable urban networks of a city, as a way of questioning simultaneously the site and the built, nature and culture, building technologies and meaning.

CHAPTER 7

Invisible cities

Paris. The city of lights. The city of dreams. The city of intellectuals. Paris has this image for all of us. Yet, Latour argued that Paris is an invisible city. 'Invisible' echoes Italo Calvino's *Invisible Cities* (1974). In a rather unorthodox book, in its design, form and style – entitled provocatively *Paris, Ville Invisible* (1998) and co-authored with photographer Emilie Hermant – Latour offered an unusual account of Paris that could be read as a pragmatist agenda for the study of cities. He set the tone of an intriguing enquiry on urban life, but also simultaneously, on social life; a tone very different in style from the one known to urban and architectural scholars. It is a book two times bigger than the usual size of a typical academic book. A book you do not simply read, but rather amble through, just like you would stroll through the large and narrow streets of a city to capture its character. Different sized fonts re-calibrate our attention to the reading; different sized images focusing on specific details of these journeys trough the city skilfully guide us through this meandering-reading. Text and visuals combine to craft the arguments reminiscent of the very crafting of urban space. From the start we are in a design register of experience, an intended effect by the authors.

Paris for millions

How many are we in the city of Paris? A Paris just for two? Like Eugène de Rastignac, famously proclaimed from the heights of the Père Lachaise Cemetery, looking down upon the faint city: 'À nous deux, maintenant!' ('It's between you and me now!'). But what if it is not a Paris just for two? But a Paris for millions? And as we find ourselves in a Paris for millions, what is it that holds us together? How are dispersed groupings assembled on such a surface? How does a city work and how, by tracing its workings, is a better understanding of social life, of togetherness obtained? These are the key questions that the Paris of Latour implies, one much different indeed from the Paris of the nineteenth-century fictional character Rastignac from the novel of Honoré de Balzac. To comprehend what defines Paris today, we commonly think of explorations of the *ego* (that is, identity, expressed with ID cards, records of civil status, testimonies by neighbours), the *hic* (that is, place, expressed as cadastral plans, maps of Paris, guidebooks, signposts) and the *nunc* (that is, time, expressed as sundials, watches, the electronic voices emitting from speaking clocks on the metro). These are three possible starting points for an exploration of the social. Yet, none of them can simply point to a Society (and a city) in which we have a role, a place and a time. Instead, 'the social' has its own movement. By 'the social', Latour designated a certain form of circulation of traces, 'a weird way of moving about, tracing figures, like unknown writing on rice paper painted with an invisible brush' (Latour and Hermant 1998, 27). To understand and to grasp Paris, we need to follow and track the 'slipping token' of the social. By so doing we never meet the acclaimed figures of the individual and the system but find ourselves following a movement that bears no relation to either actors or social contexts and *that* is the movement that Latour and Hermant invited us to follow. More specifically, there are four moves that become important: traversing, proportioning, distributing, and allowing.

<u>To understand and to grasp Paris, we need to follow and track the 'slipping token' of the social. By so doing we never meet the acclaimed figures of the individual and the system but find ourselves following a movement.</u>

Traversing

Paris is a city of totalisation. It loves its viewpoints and terraces, panoramas and vistas, reflected as if through a gallery of mirrors, seeking an all-encompassing perspective. The panoramas, as the origin of the term suggests, allow you to see *everything*. Yet, panoramas also see nothing as they only show an image painted (or projected) on the tiny wall of an enclosed room on which a completely coherent scenery is projected. The metaphor comes from those rooms invented in the early nineteenth century. Yet, none of those pictures survey 'the whole'. Latour encouraged us to forget about this obsessive totalisation, and to abandon the panoramic and 'panoptic' ways of looking at Paris (seeing the whole at one view). Forget about the heights of Montmartre or Père Lachaise where Rastignac was standing, and the Montparnasse Tower or the Eiffel Tower viewing platform! You believed that Paris can be seen from up there? But, it cannot! You thought the picture you have taken from up there *has captured* Paris as a whole, its character, its charm, its essence. But it does not! It is hard to embrace it from a distance. From the Montparnasse Tower we can barely see the Sacré Coeur basilica, from the Arc de la Défense we can barely see the silhouette of the Arc de Triomphe. All these images are partial and static, just like the projected images in those nineteenth-century cinema rooms. It becomes hard to understand what makes this big metropolitan city vibrant; each new total viewpoint blocks the previous. Paris remains invisible. Hence, Latour's proposal: 'Let's move and then, suddenly, Paris will begin to be visible'. That is *the first move: Traversing the city*. We need to stroll in the city, to meander through its streets. No big jumps, no double clicks from the top of the Eiffel Tower! We move from one visible site to another; we discover one aspect after another. Through this movement, Paris becomes progressively visible.

> **The initial point of view doesn't count; all that counts is the movement of images. All the images are partial, of course; all the perspectives are equal: that of the baby in its pram is worth as much as that of the Mairie de Paris.**
>
> **(Latour and Hermant 1998, 53)**

It is the movement that matters, not the point of departure; the movement takes us, and we follow all little transformations, without jumping or skipping a single one. The visible Paris, thus, neither resides in an isolated image (a glorious view, a postcard) nor in something external to the images (French Society, context), but in a montage of images, a circulation between different sites, a trajectory, a shaping of form, of relations that lead us elsewhere. Paris emerges in what is being transformed, transported, and deformed from one image to another, from one point of view and perspective to another. In other words, if we manage to link up, one by one, the very particular traces, traces that move rapidly, the 'slipping token' of the social, passed around, the city will become visible.

To truly see and understand Paris, we should abandon all of the sites where we talk of Paris 'as a whole' (the panoramic ones), sites where we believe we can see Paris at a glance, and focus instead on the small sites, the very *situated* perspectives, where very little of Paris can be seen, but it can be seen well. That is how Latour's Paris differs from Rastignac's Paris; he is not up there, on the hill, but rather on the ground. Those earthly sites are fundamentally invisible; they are *oligopticons*. By this neologism, constructed in opposition with panopticon, Latour designated the 'narrow windows through which, via numerous narrow channels, we can link up with only some aspects of beings (human and nonhuman) which together comprise the city' (Latour and Hermant 1998, 173). The *panopticon*, as every reader of Michel Foucault knows, is an ideal prison allowing for the total surveillance of inmates imagined at the beginning of the nineteenth century by Jeremy Bentham. Nothing, it seems, can threaten the absolutist gaze of the panopticon, and this is why it is loved so much by those sociologists who dream to occupy the centre of Bentham's prison. Yet, unlike most sociologists, instead of looking for utopia, Latour looks for places on earth that are fully assignable. The oligopticons are just those sites since they do exactly the opposite of panopticons: they see much too little ('oligo' – little, not everything), but what they see, they see it well (Figure 7.1). As Latour stated, 'to refresh a space and make it a little more realistic, it's not a map that we need, irrespective of the number of pixels, but *oligopticons*' (Latour 2011, 91).

The oligopticons are just those sites since they do exactly the opposite of panopticons: they see much too little ('oligo' – little, not everything), but what they see, they see it well (Figure 7.1).

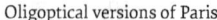
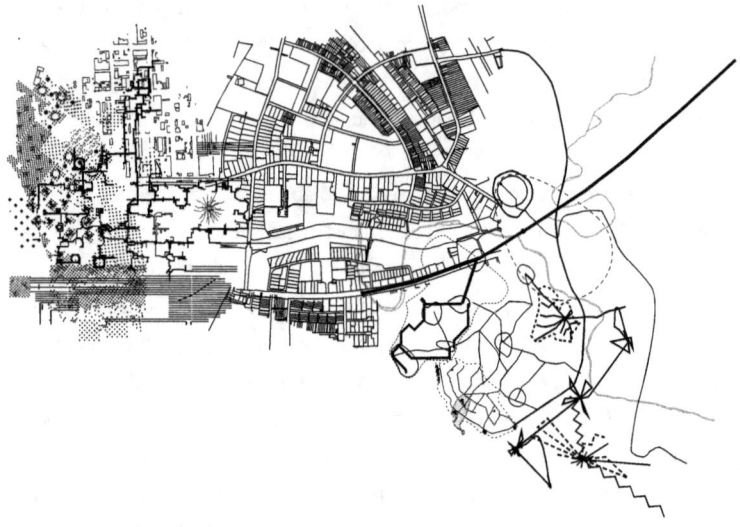

Figure 7.1 Oligoptical versions of Paris.
Illustration by Alexandra Arènes.

An oligopticon could be as big as a control panel in a closed control room. The control room can be found in the premises of water, meteorology or electricity services, in the offices of traffic control, police or telephone companies, or in the maps of town planners. From there very little can be witnessed at any time, but everything appears with great precision owing to a dual network of signs, coming and going, rising and descending, watching over Parisian life, night and day. No single control panel brings all these flows of water, electricity, telecommunication, surveillance, weather and traffic together into a single place at one time. No bird's eye view can, at a single glance, capture the multiplicity of these places and how they all add up to make the whole of Paris.

Water, electricity, telephone lines, the weather, transportation, metrology, urbanism, sociology, and police surveillance, all circulate in Paris and become visible through various oligopticons. Visit the small office of the *Service*

Parcellaire (responsible for detailed surveys), Boulevard Morland, in the 4th arrondissement. Filing cabinets line the corridors, marked with the names of neighbourhoods; follow the circulation of documents and you will begin to see invisible Paris, its streets, its exact shape. Visit the headquarters of France-Telecom, Ile-de-France and take a close look at the supervision screens, warning signals that indicate congested segments of the telephone network, skeins of coloured lines that reflect the scattered activities of millions of Parisians within the city and beyond. You begin to see Paris again. Make a stop at the famous Café de Flore on boulevard St. Germain and witness Alice paying for her coffee and the efforts of Mr Broussard, the general manager. Something that has neither the aroma nor the consistency of a little black coffee is transmuted into pure gold under his watchful eyes; here is the little jump that a coffee has to make to become a price. It is added up to the number of coffees sold, to the table numbers, to the organisation chart connecting the hectic rounds of waiters taking care of different tables, to a dispatcher, to the computer, to the taxes all Parisians should pay. It is precisely the accumulation of these little white papers, torn by the waiter when he has received the money, that the return depends on: the sum, the distribution of tips, the calculation of VAT, the payment of taxes, the weekly order of bags of coffee (a mixture skilfully prepared by the House of Vernhes for the Café de Flore). The small accounting oligopticon of Mr Broussard will lead us to another invisible Paris. Watch Mr Henry, a senior officer in the national police responsible for public safety in Paris, sitting in his office at the *Préfecture* (the central police station in Paris), with many monitors overseeing the city. At a first glace this looks like a supreme panopticon with thousands of eyes embracing the entire Paris. Yet, we only see small, specific things and sites; at the touch of a key on his computer screen he can display any of the hundred cameras on the périphérique, the Paris ring road, the two hundred videos watching over the buildings and streets of Paris, the hundreds of eyes silently patrolling the corridors of the metro. It is the aggregation of these minuscule events that produce a bigger picture. Another invisible Paris emerges. We can continue the list of oligopticons (the meteorology centre, the tube, the voting station, the research laboratories at the CNRS, etc.). The city becomes visible through the tiny channels of their networks.

None of these oligopticons are larger than 4 × 3 m. Yet, the dimension of what we look at stems not from the size of the sites but from the connections they establish and the rapidity of the circulations. Circulating everywhere, exploring the oligopticons, studying their practitioners at work, we witness how other elements of the social world emerge: water, gas, telephone, prices, stars, neurons, colonnades, wrought-iron banisters, speed bumps, votes, traffic, and fire. The term social designates what binds us together and connects us to all these beings through instruments, laboratories, templates and dossiers. The elements involved in its composition a century ago (e.g. individuals, crowds, mass movements, classes, trades, professions, cultures, structures and laws) are not the same today.

All these rare and fragile places in which the full power of the oligopticons is concentrated are situated down below, not high up, under our feet, not over our heads, or in our imagination; they are all scattered throughout the city. We can visit them, scrutinise them and account for their specificity. They prevent Paris from becoming a single block, a distant scenery seen from a hill. If we are able to study the oligopticons, it is thanks to the tracks they leave behind them, and to the closed premises that we can visit, explore, photograph and sketch. The many different interactions that constitute each of them, the entries and exists, ins and outs, makes them gain the shape of a star, a web, a fine network. And, if we studied one of the oligopticons summing up a part of the whole of Paris we would draw the same star, on the way there and on the way back. Thus,

> a city doesn't consist of a general, *stable frame* in which private actions are nestled, like doves in a dovecote or tombs in a cemetery, *but of a criss-crossing of stars*, the branches of which serve as supports, obstacles, opportunities or décor for one another, unless, as is usually the case, they never meet, even though each of them is supposed to cover the entire city.
> (Latour and Hermant 1998, 72)

Due to this versatile and starry interlaced web that emerges as we explore oligopticons, not only is it impossible to capture Paris at a glance, but it is unmanageable to grasp it from a static viewing position, taken in a moment of contemplation. Paris *is to be understood only as we move and meander* through the city and as we visit different oligopticons. Just like the social is an active engine (and not a static frame) that orders and localises, reassembles and situates, links and distinguishes, but does not have the shape of a Society, Paris is also something to be traced. Not a single spectacular panoramic picture of Paris, capturing it as a whole, but series of photos generated in these strolls, sequences in movement, running at different speeds and intensities. Through this method, one can manage to connect the traces to one another, and through the many wanderings, a figure of Paris emerges and becomes visible. Instead of offering concepts that can elucidate different features of the city, Latour's proposal is to follow the trajectories of material traces, series of transformations, and to follow them slowly in their ingenious appearance and intensity. As these traces usually remain invisible, they can be better grasped by photography (but also through sketches, diagrams, mappings, and visuals that an architecturally-informed eye can mobilise). The method proposed here is reminiscent to the architects' site visits or walks (Sorkin 2009), yet, this implies a different dynamic: a sequential visual engagement with sites and traces, a slow enquiry (Stengers 2018), a tracing of transformations on the ground. That is a pragmatist engagement with the realities of a city in all its moves.

Instead of offering concepts that can elucidate different features of the city, Latour's proposal is to follow the trajectories of material traces, series of transformations, and to follow them slowly in their ingenious appearance and intensity.

If we follow this method, we realise that in fact, *we can never see the totality of a city*. Equipped with the many eyes of cameras, notebooks, pads, sketches, mapping software, we always see a little, but we see it well. Our tools as architects-investigators constitute oligopticons similar to the other captors (questionnaires, dossiers, invoices, archives). Seeing Paris or London, Manchester or Sofia, Buenos Aires or Kuala Lampur at once becomes a pragmatic absurdity. We can only see traces, small and big, perceptible and distinct, running at different paces of speed in front of us, with us. Our images, sketches, and rough diagrams capture and magnify the movements between traces. Through their sequences, in their dance, what becomes observable is *that passage* from one visible version of the city to another that usually remains invisible.

And as we stroll and wander, capturing traces and making this passage observable, we *follow a movement* that is neither related to the context, to that stable frame of the city, nor to the individual, that famous *flâneur* who saunters around observing Society. We rather find ourselves in *a terra incognita*, a plasma, full of corridors, offices, instruments, files, rows, alignments, teams, vans, precautions, watchfulness, attention, and warnings. *Here*, we do not find a Society, following Latour, but we track *the token of the social*.

Therefore, a city does not emerge as a framework *within which* we move. Latour's proposal is different, namely, to access those channels that enable us to connect the frame with the person moving within it because the 'frame itself is made of nothing more than *traces left by other individuals* who have moved about or are still there, in place' (Latour and Hermant 1998, 30). We can understand the specificity of a city only if we are able to follow these channels, suspend the zoom, and multiply the connections between its different views.

> **In practice we never observe the move from concrete to abstract; always from *concrete to concrete*. We never leave the real for the formal, for we always slide from one real to another. Nor do we jump from the contextualized to the decontextualized, since we always wander from one institution to another.**
>
> **(Latour and Hermant 1998, 44–45).**

Thus, to see Paris or Manchester, or one of Italo Calvino's *Invisible Cities* – Armilla or Chloe, Octavia or Phyllis, Clarice, Adelma, or Berenice – we need to trace them *in concreto*. They rarely manifest themselves 'as a whole', but as a myriad of moves, disagreements, detours, and disconnected statements, whose circulation, from site to site, makes a city visible.

Proportioning

When there is a strike of metro workers, or when a bus breaks down, everyone learns quite quickly – walking, ageing and experiencing the city, just like the twin sister in the jungle – that the social world is flat and fragile, and that it requires being composed and maintained piece by piece. As we stroll in Paris, all of the sites and oligopticons appear equally flat; they connect and superimpose like spiders' webs: water, electricity, telephone, traffic networks. Impossible to distinguish what is bigger and smaller, what is the 'macro' and the 'micro', we engage in a work of putting them in relation to one another. This is *the second* important move: *Proportioning*. Instead of sticking either to *that* panoramic vision of Paris from the hill of Montmartre or *that* individual picture of the roof of Notre-Dame de Paris taken from the window of my *chambre de bonne* in the 5th arrondissement, we rather engage *in proportioning*. The work of proportioning, measuring and relating, is added to the work of tracking while traversing the city. All views of Paris are connected and superimposed like so many spider webs; there is no way they can be arranged by order of magnitude, from the encompassing to the encompassed, from the enveloping to the enveloped. The meteorological map is inter-imposed to the pollution map that laid alongside the map of the electricity network, which itself, is next to the map of the television cables; the intergalactic space produced in the Astrophysics Institute is added to that of the weather report compiled in the Météo-France offices in the Moutsouris park, which in turn is added to the map of pollution peaks published this morning in *Le Petit Parisien*. They do not overlap and cannot be reduced to each other. No camera will ever be able to zoom gradually from cable to sewer, from electricity to weather. They all matter and co-exist.

Impossible to distinguish what is bigger and smaller, what is the 'macro' and the 'micro', we engage in a work of putting them in relation to one another.

Therefore, to understand Paris it is not enough to sum them up all. When Alice is voting, from the polling booth to the ballot box, from the ballot box to the scrutineers' table, the piles of votes, counted and recounted on the black tables right up to the hall at the interior ministry's offices and, along a parallel circuit, from the opinion polls taken from the ballot boxes to the TV reports, we, *laterally*, follow channels of actions, figures, counts, and data ('obtained'), without going from small to big, from bottom to top. The same happens when we pass from the fire that has just gutted a squat in the 18th arrondissement to the Paris *Préfecture*. In fact, no tracking shot can take us from the fire straight to the police station, and the senior police officer Mr Henry is not more important than the firefighter in the 18th arrondissement. The office of the mayor of Paris is not bigger than the Café de Flore on boulevard St Germain and no bigger than my window frame. Each of them is as big as the whole of Paris. What matters is *to connect* them all, or to separate them, to aggregate them or disaggregate them. And it is this precise movement of *proportioning, or relating*, that makes Paris possible.

> The totality doesn't present itself as a fixed frame, as a constantly present context; it is obtained through a process of summing up, itself localized and perpetually restarted, whose course can be tracked. Paris is neither big nor small.
>
> (Latour and Hermant 1998, 76)

As we remain indifferent to qualifications of big and small, we witness the social threading its way between people and things without warning, connecting elements from what was previously called Nature and Society. The city is produced within the numerous oligopticons that co-exist. It is populated by crowds of people, flows of water and gas, swarms of neurons and stars, prices and votes. Yet, how can all these scattered groupings be summed up? To understand how life in the big city can be brought together, Latour shifted attention to ordinary urban objects.

Distributing

Objects and street furniture constitute an essential part of our daily environment as inhabitants that enable us to move about in the city. Here we witness *a third important move: Distributing*. Objects distribute, facilitate and enable actions. Commonly neglected, and quickly called an 'urban framework' or 'urban setting', their exclusive urbanity holds a key of common life. Kiosks, bus stops, traffic lights, ice-cream vans, mailboxes, street signs, rubbish bins, speed bumps, spikes, barriers, electronic signals, Morris columns, newsstands, theatre stands, billboards, flower booths, public toilets, bus shelters, parking metres, telephone booths, tree protectors, street names, and benches. All of these are not just objects *of* subjective passions and actions. They *do* something in the city. Through colour or form, habit or force, they bring a particular order; they attribute, authorise or prohibit, promise or permit. The bright yellow letter box makes us lift our arm, from a distance, to slip in our envelope. The bollards prohibit cars from driving onto the pavement. Tree protectors allow cyclists to chain up their bicycles and also protect the trees from damage. Transparent bins receive the rubbish in parks and allow for policemen and guards to check for their contents. Three-seat benches in the public gardens allow us to sit, but prevent homeless people from sleeping. Bus shelters provide shelter from the rain.

<u>Kiosks, bus stops, traffic lights, ice-cream vans, mailboxes, street signs, rubbish bins, speed bumps, spikes, barriers, electronic signals, Morris columns, newsstands, theatre stands, billboards,</u>

flower booths, public toilets, bus shelters, parking metres, telephone booths, tree protectors, street names, and benches. All of these are not just objects *of* subjective passions and actions. They *do* something in the city.

These urban objects are the delegates of absent forces and actors. For example, spikes, benches, and fences replace policemen, guards, and patrollers. But they make some social rules durable in the city. They have two faces: on one side, they multiply the possibility of existence of humans; on the other, they replace and multiply the occasions for them to be absent. 'Anthropogenic on the one hand; sociogenic on the other' (Latour and Hermant 1998, 107), they form this fine network that holds us together in a city by *distributing* action. All these nonhumans make it possible to share Paris and organise a particular way of living in the city together.

What tends to be invisible – the networks of water, of weather sensing, or of surveillance – become visible in situations of crisis. Objects manifest their own disobedience and unruliness: a broken bench, a spilled coffee in the metro, a damaged bike chain, an aggressive perfume in the street. The heterogeneous crowd in the city cannot be described with the simple term of intersubjectivity as if it were just happening between subjects. But it is a question of *interobjectivity*. Urban dwellers go from one object to another, from one programme of action to another. The actor strolling in the city is reminiscent of the oligopticons encountered earlier: blind but plugged in, partially intelligent, temporarily competent and locally complete. In the web of these objects, as a dweller,

> I'm neither in control nor without control: I'm formatted. I'm afforded possibilities for my existence, based on teeming devices scattered throughout the city.
>
> (Latour and Hermant 1998, 101)

Indeed, the individual is exceeded, but not by the Force of Society, that abstract force that Latour criticised in *Reassembling the Social* (2005b), but by many other beings and it is important to make sense of the multiplicity of these beings in a city. Paris is not just experienced in various subjective experiences, but is encountered in its urban interobjectivity, the tiny channels of the networks traced by urban objects.

> **In the series of transformations that we followed with myopic obsession, we would have liked to have kept each step, each notch, each stage, so that the final result could never abolish, absorb or replace the series of humble mediators that alone give it its meaning and scope.**
>
> **(Latour and Hermant 1998, 151)**

In a city that is constantly obsessed by totalisations, what could give meaning to the city are the numerous *intermediaries* that participate in the lives of millions of Parisians. As soon as we focus, not only on the traces left by paper slips and name plates, but also on the trail left by the actions of all these mediators, of iron, stone, brass and flesh, Paris is quickly overpopulated. How is it possible to hold all of this together if there is no totality to contain it from the outside, or no Social Body within which it all fits together? To make an overpopulated city work, all these networks require alignment. Standardisation is one way that makes the objects' trails easy to track. The metrology (abacus, rulers, benchmarks, patterns, standards) allows elements of the city to begin to fit together. All these constants and standards ensure that, if one wanted to measure something, one would be able to do so without the measurement changing from place to place, from time to time. This standardisation is also what holds a city together.

Allowing

Following the moves of traversing, proportioning and distributing, we gradually become aware of how overpopulated a city is, and we begin to question the social link. How do so many of us live in a city? What is it that binds us together? How can this multiplicity be explained without reverting to a structure? Addressing these questions, Latour explored how this social theory can allow and empower a different understanding of cities, of togetherness. *Here is the fourth move: Allowing.*

Two versions of Paris are possible: a cold Paris of succession, of memory, of history, and an actual Paris, an everyday Paris, a lighter city where the tight networks of surveillance cameras, electronic codes, patrols, dogs, guards and police officers no longer smothers the passer-by. Time is often defined as 'the series of successions' and space as 'the series of coexistences'. Time goes forward; space spreads out. The belief in history, in the linear series of successions has dominated social sciences, fuelling the hope that a great revolutionary gesture, a Giant Leap Forward, would sweep away the past and replace everything with a better existence. This is what constitutes a Paris of memory, of symbols, a historical Paris. But rather than understanding the city *historically*, Latour explored how a city could be grasped and defined spatially, *geographically*, as a 'series of coexistences' and not of successions. A Paris of movements *not in time*, but in connections, in networks, of oligopticons. This would mean that instead of the modernising gestures that so easily trigger succession, we would rather highlight the role of the countless intermediaries who participate in the coexistence of millions of Parisians. Economics, sociology, water, electricity, telephony, voters, geography, the climate, sewers, rumours, metros, police surveillance, standards, sums and summaries: all these circulate in Paris, through the narrow corridors of the oligopticons. They cannot serve as frame or context, because they circulate. Allowing intermediaries to be part of our world, we increase the series of coexistences. Paris is not the result of historical processes, but *constant* result of work, of maintenance, of keeping things together. And if history has ended, argued Latour, perhaps coexistence can begin.

How to study invisible cities?

In *Paris, Ville Invisible* (1998), Latour explored the actual Paris, to demonstrate that social theory can bring us closer to the city's ordinary life. In that everyday

Paris it becomes possible to meet Alice or Mr Henry in their oligopticons (rather than Picasso, Robespierre... or Balzac and his fictional character Rastignac). If we overlook Mr. Broussard's work at Café de Flore, for instance, economy seems to be a mysterious force; if we lose sight of the polling booth of Alice and the ballot box, the scrutineers and the pollsters, national representations remain an abstraction detached from everything. If we disregard the painstaking labour of the National Bureau of Standards, we believe that the whole world always consists of equal and uniform things. Instead of mysterious detached forces, the specific practices that produce actual Paris become visible.

Such accounts produced ethnographically can better capture the practical relations between the macro scale and the modification of human and nonhuman associations. A better understanding of cities could be gained by literally keeping our compass sights on the paths through the city, on the paths into and out of it, following the routes that link humans with the natural world, the subjective with the objective, the built with the unbuilt, the small with the big. To miss following these traces and accounting for these paths is to miss what the city is. Trace urban processes and ecologies (i.e. design developments, unfolding urban controversies and disputes), suspend the zoom, multiply the adjunctions between different statements, re-localise the sites where one talks about a city, and you will see an invisible city that is to be composed, recollected, and aggregated. Cities will emerge as pertinent ethnographic objects, as traceable, describable and accountable (Doucet 2015; Jensen 2014; Kärrholm 2007; Yaneva 2011; Zitouni 2010).

<u>A better understanding of cities could be gained by literally keeping our compass sights on the paths through the city, on the paths into and out of it, following the routes that</u>

link humans with the natural world, the subjective with the objective, the built with the unbuilt, the small with the big.

This approach can inspire urban scholars and designers to perfect their 'art of describing' cities, and to produce accounts that trace and measure the flow and multiplicity of urban life without replacing the specific with the general, the concrete with the abstract. This can also allow us to reinvent the narrative techniques that help us gain access to the particular and grasp the unique. Equipped with various tools of description, both discursive and visual, the accounts of urban scholars and design practitioners informed and inspired by Latour's philosophy, should deploy cities as networks, instead of unveiling in a critical fashion, what is behind them: the cultural, political, economic or social forces at work. To deploy means to account for the socio-material work of the thousands of architects, engineers, planners, policemen, meteorologists, civil servants and inhabitants, performed in many oligopticons, that make a city visible. Thus, a Latourian approach places both architectural research and practice right *within the heart* of urban life.

CHAPTER 8

The parliament of things

As in his discussions of modernity, science, technology, space and the city – and putting aside the division between Nature and Society – Latour suggested a different understanding of politics (the way we can keep order in society). Politics, to him, is no longer one realm of action separated from the others; it does not refer to the manner in which individuals seek to influence and control others in large social groups as this limits its understanding to human interests only. Instead, argued Latour, politics in contemporary life should be discussed in reference to the nonhuman world. As controversial facts multiply, and scientific controversies proliferate, the voices of nonhumans should be taken into account too. Therefore, 'politics is made not with politics but with something else' (Latour 1988a, 56). Nonhumans actively contribute to this new political regime, renewing the political game from top to bottom with new forces. Dealing with the practical work of the sciences – as an alternative to a Science with capital 'S' – will provide the possibility of building another type of democracy, one that:

> **can only be conceived if it can freely traverse the now dismantled border between science and politics, in order to add a series of new voices to the discussion, voices that have been inaudible up to now, although their clamour pretended to override all debate:** *the voices of nonhumans.*
>
> (Latour 2004b, 69)

<u>Politics in contemporary life should be discussed in reference to the nonhuman world.</u>

Therefore, democracy cannot be established, according to Latour, by simply defending the rights of the human subject to speak on behalf of others but should include the voices of nonhumans. Of course, this does not mean that things speak 'on their own', since nothing has the capacity to speak on its own, but always through something or someone else, through intermediaries or mediators. Millions of subtle mechanisms coming from the sciences are capable of adding new voices to the chorus of public life. Thus, refusing to restrict politics to humans, subjects, or 'freedom', on the one hand, and Science to objects, nature and 'necessity', on the other, we will be able to follow the work of 'stirring the entities of the collective together in order to make them articulable and to *make them speak*' (Latour 2004b, 89), procedures common both to politics and to the sciences. Thus, politics, in Latourian terms, is what allows many heterogeneous resources to be woven together into a social link that becomes increasingly harder to break (just like the microbes at the time of Pasteur redefined what society is made up of, who acts and how). It makes central the process by which the cosmos is collected into one liveable whole.

Politics is no longer framed inside the modernist settlement of Nature (understood as unified and indisputable) and Society (disputable), between the mute things of the epistemological tradition (the things to be represented) and the speaking subject of the political tradition (the one who speaks on behalf of citizens). If we follow the formation of collectives, we need to dissociate the notion of external reality from that of indisputable necessity, in order to be able to distribute it equally among all humans and nonhumans. Thus, politics is about the 'progressive composition of one common world' (Latour 2004b, 18), a way to 'redefine science and politics and to carry out the task of political epistemology forced upon us by the various ecological crises' (Latour 2005b, 254). Politics leads to the creation of a *parliament of things*.

> However, we do not have to create this Parliament out of whole cloth, by calling for yet another revolution. We simply have to ratify what we have always done, provided that we reconsider our past, provided that we understand retrospectively to what extent we have never been modern, and provided that we re-join the two halves of the symbol broken by Hobbes and Boyle as a sign of recognition. Half of our politics is constructed in science and technology. The other half of Nature

is constructed in societies. Let us patch the two back together, and the political task can begin again.

(Latour 1993a,144)

Parliament is a technical term for Latour that indicates the political act of *making things public*, a way of producing voices and connections among people. In the parliament of things, scientists talk on behalf of natures and politicians talk on behalf of citizens and societies, both doubting the faithfulness of these representatives and their representations. In parliament, there are no naked truths, on one hand, and naked citizens, on the other. Instead, the mediators, the imbroglios and networks have the whole space to themselves. And, most importantly, *they are the ones that have to be represented*; it is around them that the parliament of things gathers. And if the job of the philosopher is to explain the need for such a gathering, 'others will be able to convene the Parliament of Things' (Latour 1993a, 145). These could be artists, designers, architects or other art professionals. Their varied expertise is needed to better visualise the procedures of parliamentary assent and dissent.

Object-oriented politics

Mobilising their expertise, Latour engaged in an experiment in 'thing politics' (or *Dingpolitik* in German) on the occasion of the ZKM exhibit 'Making Things Public' in Germany, curated in collaboration with Peter Weibel (2005c). By *Dingpolitik*, he designates 'a risky and tentative set of experiments in probing just what it could mean for political thought to turn "things" around and to become slightly more realistic than has been attempted up to now' (Latour 2005c, 14). Advocating what might be called an object-oriented politics, Latour argued that, in reality, we are all more connected to each other by our worries, our matters of concern, the issues we care for, than by any other set of values, opinions, attitudes or principles. People assemble around things, around 'pragma'. And yet, politics in its traditional forms is still based on subjective opinions, passions, and abstract procedures. In an object-oriented politics, then, each object – each issue – generates a different pattern of emotions and disruptions, of disagreements and agreements. Each object triggers new occasions to passionately differ and dispute. Each object gathers around itself a different assembly of relevant parties that forms a public around it. All publics need to be represented, authorised, legitimated and brought to bear inside the relevant assembly. Therefore, an object-oriented politics and democracy is needed to detect the relevant parties and the methods to bring things into the centre of the debate. New ways of assembling and representing things are also required. A new political eloquence is needed too; this will imply bringing the objects in the political debate, into different kinds of representations that seek to make them speak loudly, politically.

New ways of assembling and representing things are also required. A new political eloquence is needed too.

For too long, objects have been wrongly portrayed as matters of fact. Yet how often do we encounter transparent, unmediated, and stable facts? It is hard to provide indisputable proof, to convince publics of the presence of a controversial phenomenon or of a looming danger. Instead, more and more, we are confronted with disputed facts, or *matters of concern*, issues that draw us together. *Matters of concern*, as a term, points to highly uncertain and loudly discussed, real, atypical and interesting agencies, that are taken as gatherings (and not as objects). We assemble around such disputed facts, not because we agree, but because these divisive matters of concern bring us together. That is the reason why Latour revived the old meaning of the word 'Thing' (or the Latin *res*) that for many centuries has recalled the issue that brings people together because it divides them. He suggested to bring things back to the political arena as politics has been for long emptied of things and filled only with human passions, beliefs and values. The *res*, the thing, designates both those who assemble because they are concerned as well as what causes their concerns and divisions. Bringing things into politics however disrupts our traditional spaces or forms of politics. They will, instead, create hybrid forums, spaces of conflict and negotiation between actors (Callon, Lascoumes and Barthes 2011), a parliament

of things. These are spaces in which various groups can meet and debate
different issues and the technical choices of importance to the community. They
are hybrid, moreover, because the people involved and their representatives are
heterogeneous: experts, politicians, and concerned lay people. Hybrid, also,
because the questions to be tackled are of a different nature: from political and
ethical concerns through to technical and scientific. Bringing things into these
hybrid forums creates new kinds of gatherings of humans and nonhumans, new
ways of associating. Reflecting on the importance of an object-oriented politics
(Joerges 1999; Winner 1980) in architecture can bring new awareness to the
ways in which global infrastructure networks can become mediums of politics
(Easterling 2014), architecture can be political at the level of design, construction
and inhabitation practices (Yaneva 2017; Mommersteeg 2020), and to the
different architectural and urban sites of political action (Jaque 2020).

Cosmos and cosmopolitics

The scale of ecological crises, Latour claimed, forced us to realise that politics has
always been object-oriented and that every kind of politics has always been a
*cosmo*politics, a politics of the cosmos, a politics that turns around the question
of what our common world consists of (Latour 2005c). To designate the
politics of a cosmos, Latour (and Isabelle Stengers (2010a, 2010b)) introduced
the term *cosmopolitics*, which differs from cosmopolitanism. Cosmopolitan,
cosmopoliticum, is a very old term, that comes from the ancient philosophy
of the Stoics and Immanuel Kant's theory of international relations, which
designates historically the citizenship of those who pertain to the world, to
the networks of the great cities, and to the need for a common global culture
and a universal citizenship. For this philosophical tradition of cosmopolitanism,
the individual is a global citizen of the world which might become their polis
(cosmopolis). In this form of European internationalism, moreover, nature and
the cosmos, is unified, singular, and without history. Issues of war and peace
involve a struggle between different views of and perspectives *on* the world.
Cosmopolitanism is thereby a desire to reach a global consensus of perspectives,
a coming-together of cultures.

In contrast, in the cosmopolitical perspective of Stengers and Latour, the *cosmos* is indeterminate and uncertain. It, itself, is an object of politics. Nature, or the cosmos, is no longer unified enough to provide a stabilising pattern for the experience of humans, or a 'standard' from which to judge political questions, to agree to a consensus. It is not 'out there', a simple passive backdrop for human activities. Instead, it is to be done, created, instigated; it is to be 'composed' (Latour 2010b). Isabelle Stengers offered a sophisticated reading of the term cosmopolitics (Stengers 2010a, 2010b) by representing it as a composite of the strongest meaning of cosmos and the strongest meaning of politics. The cosmopolitical proposal has nothing to do with the miracle of decisions that 'put everyone into agreement' as the dispute is inside every single discipline and no longer between the natural sciences (Nature) and the social sciences (Society, Culture). To generate cosmopolitics it is not enough to add a political interpretation to genes or to glare, to take some examples. Instead, genes and glare are complex matters of concern. In genetics there is already a wide discussion among biologists regarding what a gene actually is and means. Architects and engineers engage in endless discussions on how to calculate and mitigate the effects of glare, as seen in our introductory example. There are therefore much more entities to be taken into account. Once we extend the range of entities our world is made of, as they all have to form a liveable collective, politics enters the scene as a procedure through which decisions are made about what entities our world should be composed of. We, therefore, need to introduce political interpretations into the definitions of natural sciences, and things into politics so as to be able to achieve a progressive composition of the common world (Figure 8.1).

Therefore, citizens of the world may be cosmopolitan, global, and tolerant to different cultures, but this does not mean that they have even begun to grasp the difficulties of a politics of the cosmos. In situations of conflict, not only cultures but the entire cosmos is in jeopardy. To see and understand this, we must cultivate an anthropological sensitivity, Latour argued, in order to witness and experience the variations of nature. Thus, whereas in cosmopolitan thinking there is one Nature and the cosmos is unified, in cosmopolitics nature is multiplied; it appears in different variations: *a pluriverse* (a term

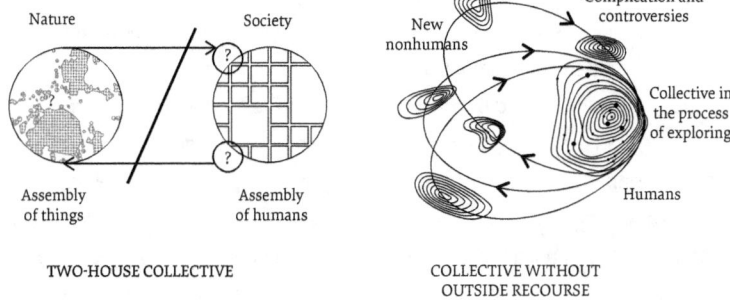

Figure 8.1 The political model with two houses; The model of the collective. Illustration by Alexandra Arènes.

borrowed from the American pragmatist philosopher William James (1996) and coined in opposition of *universe*). While cosmopolitan thinkers reflect on the characteristics and the 'subject' of the cosmopolitan age at the beginning of the third millennium, the preoccupation of cosmopolitical scholars is rather different: to open up to the diversity of the world and to acknowledge the existence of all the entities composing it.

Cosmopolitical design

Abandoning the modernist idea of Nature as external to human experience – a Nature that can be mastered by engineers and scientists from the outside – Latour invited us to embrace a different, a non-modern attitude to it that will require an active process of manipulating and reworking it 'from within'. This brings the question of making, of design, to the fore. Arguing that there is a very strong connection between the word cosmos and the word design, Latour asked: what is cosmopolitical design? What does it mean to be cosmopolitically correct? Cosmos is a term that designates the aesthetically and morally comfortable ordering of things. Connecting entities into a liveable assemblage is not enough; but, and this is the political question for Latour, they should also be composed in order to design one common world. Thus, key Latourian questions – like How many are we? How can we live together? How do we assemble aggregates of humans and nonhumans to form a liveable world? – must be tackled by the various skills of scientists, politicians, artists, moralists, economists, legislators, but also, architects, and designers. If we are to be 'cosmopolitically correct' as Latour suggested (Latour 2007b), we need to portray the zone between the natural and the social sciences and reinvent them both. We need to build and deploy the hybrid networks, the imbroglios, caused by ecological mutations, by scientific inventions, by resource extractions, etc., and to reinvent both politics and the arts to be able to fully apprehend these complex transformations and contribute to change.

Key Latourian questions – like How many are we? How can we live together? How do we assemble aggregates of humans and nonhumans to form a liveable world? – must be tackled by the various skills of scientists, politicians, artists, moralists, economists, legislators, but also, architects, and designers.

The meaning of cosmopolitics is better grasped in concrete situations where practitioners operate. Following Latour, therefore, we can ask what the role of design is in this new cosmopolitical regime. How do designers make explicit the connections of humans to a variety of entities with different ontologies: rivers, species, particles? How is the agency of other species and objects taken into account and the political order redefined? Engaging with these cosmopolitical questions, architects have begun devising responses through interdisciplinary dialogues and practices (Yaneva and Zaera-Polo 2015). To engage in cosmopolitics means to redesign every single feature of our common experience, both the cosmos and the political assemblies. Architects, therefore, can act *from within*, raising awareness of the effects of climate change, and offering new compositions, new local adjustments that would craft the cosmos differently without resorting to political speeches or activism.

Therefore, as a cosmopolitical practice, design becomes the activity of those who cannot any longer count on a unified Nature and engages in entirely reordering the material and living world. A natural park in the Alps, for instance, is no longer a natural environment 'out there' waiting to be discovered by visitors and defended by militant environmentalists (Mauz and Gravelle 2005). Instead, it is entirely designed and reshaped right down to the behaviour of wolves and mountain goats, tourists and hunters, vegetation and ecological organisations. Far from being a passive Nature, it is an assembly of cultures and natures, that is to be redesigned by all those who have relevant knowledge and who constantly perform adjustments 'from within'. Thus, there is an important distinction between political and cosmopolitical ecology. Political ecology affirms that all knowledge is objectively produced and verified by experts. Politics is commonly reduced to a verbal game, leaving astray all the entities that both contribute to producing or destroying our worlds: nonhumans like viruses, natural disasters, climate, carbon dioxide, floods, rivers, and so on. However, when there is 'an issue that not only does not allow itself to be dissociated in fact-value terms, but also needs to be given the power to activate thinking among those who have relevant knowledge about it' (Stengers 2005, 1002), we are in the regime of cosmopolitical ecology. A cosmopolitical perspective acknowledges that there is no 'objective definition' of a virus or a flood that everyone will share, a standard outside of situated engagements with them. A detached definition of those entities accepted by all would not produce a better understanding of the world transformed by viruses or floods. Instead, we need to account for the active participation of all those whose practice effectively engages in multiple modes 'with' the virus or 'with' the river. The cosmopolitical ecology, advocated by Latour, embraces all the objects of human and nonhuman collective life bearing on complicated forms of association between beings – regulations, equipment, consumers, institutions, habits, calves, rivers, cows, pigs, and floods. 'Ecology/ to ecologise' has thus become the plausible alternative to 'modernisation/ to modernise': a new way to handle all the objects of human and nonhuman collective life (Latour 1998) which require a new form of political activity adapted to the study of their networks.

> **In practice, politicians have never dealt with humans, but always with associations of humans and nonhumans, cities and landscapes, productions and diversions, things and people, genes and properties, goods and attachments, in brief *cosmograms*.**
>
> (Latour 2004b, 145)

The cosmogram (Tresch 2005, 2007) is an image of a world in which one wants to live. Confronted with the challenges of the Anthropocene, architecture is required more than ever to address the primordial question of what it means to live together in peace, and thus to design new cosmograms, to imagine and speculate about new forms of co-existence between humans and nonhumans, of how to share a common world. Architectural design can contribute to reshaping the co-existence of different entities, and ultimately to the re-architecting of the cosmos. Latour's philosophy invites us to rethink the role of design in the new climatic regime of planetary thinking.

CHAPTER 9

A Gaia who cares

The intrusion of Gaia

Confronted by the ecological crisis and the mutations of the Earth and our leaving conditions, we, humans, feel so powerless. What does it mean to be morally responsible at the time of the Anthropocene, when the Earth is shaped by us, when we have become a geological force, by our irresponsibility, a disregard for the consequences of our actions, uneven consequences that are difficult to grasp, to locate, to pin down… and that even the loop connecting our collective action to its consequence is thrown into doubt? This climate question is, according to Latour, at the heart of all geopolitical issues: 'all forms of belonging are undergoing metamorphosis – belonging to the globe, to the world, to the provinces, to particular plots of ground, to the world market, to lands or to traditions' (Latour 2018b, 16). Migrations, increasing inequality, environmental and social injustice, and this new climatic regime are one and the same threat. The global pandemic of 2020 also confirmed Latour's fears, which played out as a rehearsal for what is to come:

> **The first lesson the coronavirus has taught us is also the most astounding: we have actually proven that it is possible, in a few weeks, to put an economic system on hold everywhere in the world and at the same time, a system that we were told it was impossible to slow down or redirect. To every ecologist's argument about changing our ways of life, there was always the opposing argument about the irreversible force of the 'train of progress' that nothing could derail 'because of globalisation', they would say. And yet it is precisely its globalised character that makes this infamous development so fragile, so likely to do the opposite and come to a screeching halt.**
>
> (Latour 2020, 1)

This climate question is, according to Latour, at the heart of all geopolitical issues.

This moment of the global ecological crisis has disturbed how we, as humans, understand our place in the world and in history: it has been described as the 'end of history', or positions us at the 'ends of the world', disrupting how we understand our *finality* and finitude; but it has also made us rethink how humans relate to others, or what it means to be human at all, qualified as 'post-human'. But Latour has gone so far as to call it 'post-natural' as Nature is no longer what is embraced from a faraway point of view where the observer could ideally jump to see things 'as a whole', but is an assemblage of contradictory entities that have to be composed together. Just like the category of the 'human', the category of 'Nature' does not adequately correspond to this state of affairs. In place of Nature, Latour, building from the hypothesis formulated by the chemist James Lovelock and microbiologist Lynn Margulis – that living organisms interact with their inorganic surroundings on Earth to form a self-regulating complex system that maintains the conditions for life on the planet – offered the figure of Gaia (Latour 2017b). Gaia is named after the primordial goddess who personified the Earth in Greek mythology and the spirit of our planet. Unlike Nature, Gaia is not indifferent; she is local, she cares and feels for us, reacts to us, and might, eventually, get rid of us. Gaia *as a figure* allows us to not de-animate Nature as Gaia undoubtedly acts and reacts. However, Gaia is *also* a scientific concept that seeks to capture the 'living Earth' as a reciprocal and entangled relationship of various entities that each have their own interests, and importantly for Latour, without imposing a totality over them. Gaia is a secular figure for Nature, and has no place in the Nature–Culture schema. She is neither ontologically unified, nor a super-organism endowed with a unified agency, and that is why she is politically interesting:

> I should like to insist on two particularly surprising characteristics of Gaia: first, that it is composed of agents that are neither de-animated nor

over-animated; then, contrary to what Lovelock's detractors claim, that it is made up of agents that are not prematurely unified in a single acting totality. Gaia, the outlaw, is the anti-system.

(Latour 2017a: 87)

Following Lovelock and Margulis's thesis, Latour argued that something has been totally overlooked when the Earth is considered from the outside (as in Galileo's discovery that the Earth moved around the Sun). Earth *as* Gaia is incredibly reactive to our actions, not only that the Earth moves around the Sun but that it is being moved by us, modified from within, and 'for that reason escapes all our hopes of dominating it' (Latour 2018a, 223) compared to Nature which was seemingly indifferent to our actions, and for that reason could be mastered. The limited, restricted, local, active, and reactive Gaia is freed from the concept of Nature. Latour's thinking on nature developed in *Politics of Nature* (2004b) gained a different direction with Gaia. Gaia is the occasion for a return to Earth that allows for a differentiated version of earthbound sciences, politics, and religions. Whether we are dealing with the idea of the Anthropocene, the theory of Gaia, or the notions of historical actors like Humanity or Nature taken as a whole, the danger is always the same: we have the temptation to *explain* everything within a coherent and unified whole.

<u>Earth *as* Gaia is incredibly reactive to our actions, not only that the Earth moves around the Sun but that it is being moved by us, modified from within, and 'for that reason escapes all our hopes of dominating it' (Latour 2018a, 223) compared to Nature which was seemingly indifferent to our actions, and for that reason could be mastered.</u>

Latour distinguished between the concepts of Land and Globe, both of which are wholly different both scientifically and politically. 'The figure of the Globe authorises a premature leap to a higher level by confusing the figures of connection with those of totality' (Latour 2017a: 130). The Globe with a capital 'G' simultaneously delineates scientific, economic, and moral horizons, the Globe of globalisation (Figure 9.1). Under the Globe of globalisation what had to be abandoned in order to modernise was the Local, the Land. When we move forward to the Globe, we are considered progressive, in all senses of the world (Left); and when we move backward toward the land, we are considered reactionary (Right).

Yet, if we consider the planet as a Globe, this means that we imagine ourselves in some sort of godlike position. A view from nowhere. It is from this imaginary viewpoint that we can consider local attachments to the Land, to the 'Heimat', as limited, regressive, and archaic (the recent rise of the far-right in Europe or Trumpism in the USA witnessed for this trend). For us, those 'who live on the land surveyed by this all-powerful gaze, the Globe appears as an infinite horizon,

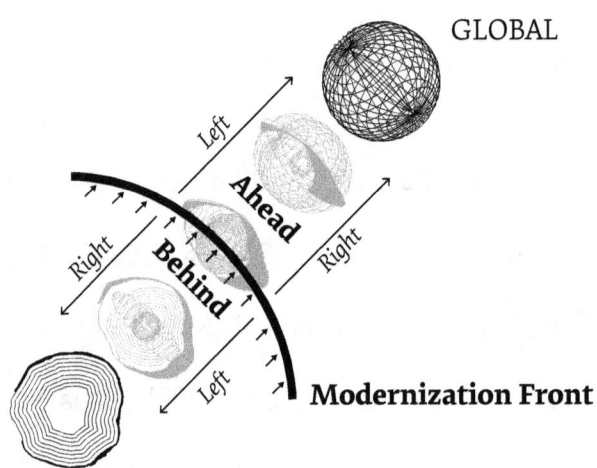

Figure 9.1 Modernisation front between global and local.
Illustration by Alexandra Arènes.

an always-receding frontier' (Latour 2018a, 219). Instead, Latour advocated stepping out of this modernist schema. To move sideways from the traditional Left–Right distinction in politics, away from the progressive idealism of the Globe and globalisation and the regressive belief in naturalism, land, and identity, the Local, towards a third option, to return back down to the Earth, the Gè, Gaia. Gaia confers freedom to entities which were confined to the natural framework before, granting them the ability to create their own living conditions (Latour and Lenton 2019). For each phenomenon in Gaia, a vast array of practitioners has alternative views of what those entities are and how they should behave. This newly drawn cosmological domain of Gaia is not a place for epistemological peace, of consensus, of unification, but of epistemological dispute. If we ask a farmer what he or she thinks of agronomy, an Amerindian of what he or she thinks of modern agroforestry, a worker of a bank what he or she thinks of the law of economics, we will find out that their relevant knowledge gained within these fields of practice matters, that the consensus of experts can no longer be the judge to resolve our disputes and that 'no discipline any longer has the power to disqualify those claims' (Latour 2018a, 224).

This newly drawn cosmological domain of Gaia is not a place for epistemological peace, of consensus, of unification, but of epistemological dispute.

It is important, stated Latour, that we step aside and find 'a place to land' in order to escape the front of modernisation. There is nothing that authorises us to re-use the old markers of politics such as 'Right' and 'Left', 'liberation', 'emancipation', 'market forces', or even the markers of space and time that have appeared self-evident for so long, the 'Local' or 'Global', 'future' or 'past'. Everything requires being mapped out anew and at new costs. This is an urgent task that must be carried out before we rush forward, and lose what we care about. We need to take stock of what matters to us, of what we are attached to, to develop a balance-sheet of where we are at (*cahiers de doléances*, a list of grievances).

Redirecting attention from Nature towards the Earth, Gaia or the Terrestrial, we need to ask ourselves: 'Are we Moderns or Terrestrials?' (Latour 2018b, 55). In this way, we can begin to apprehend more clearly the premises of a new affect that would reorient the forces at work in a lasting way. This might also put an end to 'the disconnect that has frozen political positions since the appearance of the climate threat and has imperilled the linking of the so-called social struggles with those we call ecological' (Latour 2018b, 82). We cannot act politically, argued Latour, without having surveyed and measured, being by being, person by person, the stuff that makes up the Earth for us. Now more than ever, alternative descriptions, accounts and visualisations of the Earth need to be generated. This would also mean engaging in local experiments (Latour and Weibel 2020) in what it means to inhabit an Earth after modernisation, with all those, humans and nonhumans, displaced and affected by its course. These collaborative experimental projects with artists are important to address the environmental crisis as the arts offer a variety of modes of description through theatre, visual arts, design, and architecture. The School for Political Arts established by Latour at Sciences-Po (SPEAP) is an example for such an interdisciplinary endeavour.

Architectural contributions to Gaia-graphy

Reflecting on the new climatic regime, designers can help produce alternative descriptions of the Earth. An ambitious agenda for architecture at the time of Anthropocene can be set: to rethink design through a theory of human and material coexistence. Designers are the first to test different ways of assembling, harmonising and re-composing the world; they can also rethink techniques, sites, scales, and aesthetic devices to acknowledge the agency of entities and the relationships among them.

An ambitious agenda for architecture at the time of Anthropocene can be set: to rethink design through a theory of human and material coexistence.

A new politics of the cosmos is possible only if we can represent intricate, complicated environmental issues (climate change, soil degradation, threats to biodiversity) in their multiple scales, gravity, and durations; designers can provide new representational tools and tactics. For this aim, Latour has engaged in collaborations with architects and geochemists to study the Earth's surface: a porous zone affected by life and modified by geochemical cycles, a thin pellicle, a few kilometres thick, called the Critical Zone (Arènes, Latour and Gaillardet 2018). Situating their analysis at the Critical Zone, where the biosphere, hydrosphere, lithosphere and atmosphere all meet, designers can make visible the interactions between various forms of life, matter, and landscape, as well as the disturbances caused by humans and nonhumans, and their various chemical residues (Arènes 2022). If modernist thinkers conceived of the globe as a celestial machine, that can be seen from nowhere and grasped *in toto*, the Earth Sciences understand it in a very different way: as a layered, organic system. Offering an anamorphosis, a distortion of the Earth image, different from the dominating planetary view, known since the 'Scientific Revolution', Latour and his collaborators shifted the representation from a planetary vision of sites located in the cartographic grid to a 'Gaia-graphic view' in order to embed viewers within diverse zones of biological concentration, the microcosmos where the Earth's layers can be explored, and their fragility made visible (Figure 9.2).

The lack of a common visual language hampers the understanding of environmental issues such as the rapid degradation of landscapes or the massive stores of pollution in our atmosphere, sea or soil at the time of the Anthropocene. Conventional cartographic, scientific, and cybernetic images speak in an abstracted, top-down totalising aesthetic. The difficulty of visualising and comprehending the conditions of environmental transformation has also contributed to climate change scepticism and denial. Latour urged us, therefore, to rethink the representational techniques that have for long shaped how we look at nature, and to multiply the instruments for data collection and representation. Inspired by Latour's ideas on the new climatic regime, architects Rania Ghosn and El Hadi Jazairy (2018), for instance, use inventive mapping techniques to trace the Earth zones affected by acute environmental issues through the rubrics of dynamic processes and physiologies (Figure 9.3). Their

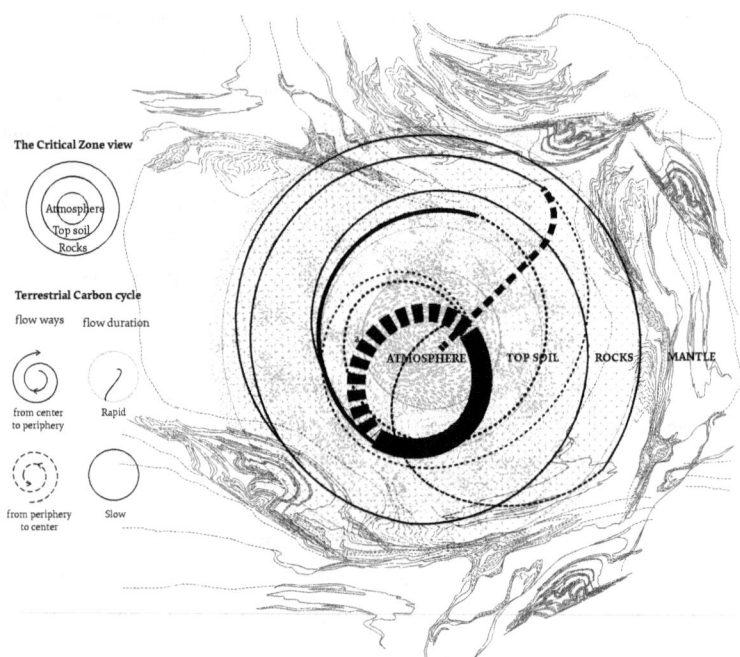

Figure 9.2 A visualisation of the Critical Zone.
Illustration by Alexandra Arènes.

'geostories' take us into the thick of the Earth: into the middle of the ocean, of oil extraction infrastructure, melting icebergs, and waste management. Addressing critical questions of deforestation and resource extraction, these parliaments of things are very different from the purified concept of the Globe and the romantic Nature. They also seek to rethink multispecies cohabitation and make explicit the fragile connections between humans and nonhumans with different ontologies.

Redefining the traditional cartographic techniques, architects in collaboration with science studies scholars adapted their representational methods (Aït-Touati, Arènes and Grégoire 2019). Thanks to these collaborations new powerful cosmograms (Ohanian and Royoux 2004; Sloterdijk, 2005, 2016; Tresch 2005,

Figure 9.3 DESIGN EARTH, 'Frozen Record', Of Oil and Ice, 2017.
Credit: 'Design Earth'.

2007) have been developed; cosmograms that establish a shared understanding of the components that constitute Gaia. They craft new compositions, new layers, new interlocking swarms of actors and technologies in inverted scales, overlapping niches and novel envelopes, and new 3D visualisations that mirror these fragile webs of connections. Through these visual analyses, the Earth appears as layered, composed of complex biological and geological entities, instruments and techniques, and always seen in three dimensions, and from different perspectives. The designers' techniques offer a continuous embedding in the ever-multiplied folds of this multi-layered, and ever-surprising, Earth.

This new regime of visualisation suggests that we live *within* Gaia and interact with it, that we weave a web of connections that might hurt or repair its balance. Instead of geography, an inventive Gaia-graphy is at stake, which can reveal the composition of troubled territories and actively trace the moves of Gaia within them. In these visualisations the human does not appear as a separate layer on top of other geological or biological phenomena, but rather as a switch, a shape shifter among the other phenomena. Mapping and visualising the 'intrusions of Gaia' (Stengers 2015) in politics in a compelling way requires the intelligence of the analytical and visual tactics that are so essential to architecture. At a time when both the concepts of Globe and Land are scientifically and politically loaded, Latour's invitation to move sideways and explore, account, and visualise the Earth could offer a unique opportunity for architects to register the earthly mappings of Gaia's moves. As such, Latour's philosophy can promote a new role for architectural design: as a powerful apparatus for re-diagramming, re-thinking and re-imagining a new cosmopolitical order.

Latour's invitation to move sideways and explore, account, and visualise the Earth could offer a unique opportunity for architects to register the earthly mappings of Gaia's moves.

This charts without any doubt, a future shaped by a radically new engagement of designers with the environmental issues and the fate of the planet Earth. As Latour famously stated, 'Neither Nature nor the Others will become modern. It is up to us to change our ways of changing' (Latour 1993a, 145). There is no better way of concluding this book than by extending an invitation to architects and design scholars to read and engage with the philosophical oeuvre of this earthly giant, hoping this will inspire new designerly ways to change our ways of changing.

Further reading

In addition to reading the selection of Bruno Latour's works cited in this book and the series of ethnographies of architectural practices that followed suit, I would recommend reading a short article of Latour, initially delivered as a keynote lecture, where he addressed explicitly issues of design and invention that might be relevant for architects and scholars in design studies:

Latour, B. 2008. 'A Cautious Prometheus? A Few Steps Toward a Philosophy of Design (with special attention to Peter Sloterdijk)', Paper presented at Networks of Design Meeting of Design History Society Falmouth, Cornwall, 3 September 2008.

For those interested in the philosophical aspects of Latour's work, read:

Latour, B. 2013. *An Inquiry Into the Modes of Existence: An Anthropology of the Moderns*. MA: Harvard University Press. For readers curious to hear more about Actor-Network-Theory as a method, read: Law, J. and Hassard, J., eds., 1999. *Actor Network Theory and After*. Oxford: Blackwell.

For those interested in how some of Latour's ideas have travelled to the field of planning, the work of Jonathan Metzger provides excellent insights:

Metzger J. 2016. 'Cultivating Torment: The Cosmopolitics of More-Than-Human Urban Planning', *City* 20(4): 581–601.

In geography, the work of Valerie November could be useful for architects:

November, V., Camacho-Hubner, E. and Latour, B. 2010. 'Entering Risky Territory – Space in the Age of Digital Navigation', *Environment and Planning D* 28(4): 581–599.

Finally, for readers curious to learn more about the ways the global pandemic that unfolded in 2020 has affected humans, cities and territories and made us rethink issues of globalisation and climate change, read:

Latour, B. 2021. *After Lockdown: A Metamorphosis*. London: Wiley.

Bibliography

Aït-Touati, F., Arènes, A. and Grégoire, A. 2019. *Terra Forma: FORMA*. Manuel de cartographies potentielles. Paris: Éditions B42.

Akrich, M. 1992. 'The De-scription of Technical Objects', in *Shaping Technology/Building Society: Studies in Sociotechnical Change*, edited by W.E. Bijker and J. Law, 205–224. Cambridge, MA: MIT Press.

Akrich, M. and Latour, B. 1992. 'A Summary of a Convenient Vocabulary for the Semiotics of Human and Nonhuman Assemblies', in *Shaping Technology-Building Society: Studies in Sociotechnical Change*, edited by W. Bijker and J. Law, 259–264. Cambridge, MA: MIT Press.

Akrich, M., Callon, M. and Latour, B. 2002. 'The Key to Success in Innovation, Part I: The Art of Interessement', *International Journal of Innovation Management* 6(2): 187–206.

Albertsen, N. and Dicken, B. 2004. 'Artworks' Networks: Field, System of Mediators?', *Theory, Culture and Society* 21(3): 35–58.

Arènes, A. 2022. 'Architectural Design at the Time of Anthropocene: A Gaia-graphic Approach to the Critical Zones', PhD Dissertation, University of Manchester.

Arènes, A., Latour, B. and Gaillardet, J. 2018. 'Giving Depth to the Surface: An Exercise in the Gaia-graphy of Critical Zones', *The Anthropocene Review* 5(2): 120–135.

Armando, A. and Durbiano, G. 2017. *Teoria del progetto architettonico: dai disegni agli effetti*. Roma: Carocci.

Blackwell, B. 2022. 'Building a Graphene City: Infrastructuring a New Scientific Ecology', PhD Dissertation, University of Manchester.

Blok, A. and Jensen, T.E. 2011. *Bruno Latour: Hybrid Thoughts in a Hybrid World*. London and New York: Routledge.

Borch, C. 2008. 'Foam Architecture: Managing Co-isolated Associations', *Economy and Society* 37(4): 548–571.

Bouzarovski, S. 2015. *Retrofitting the City: Residential Flexibility, Resilience and the Built Environment*. London and New York: I.B. Tauris.

Bucciarelli, L. 1994. *Designing Engineers*. Cambridge, MA: MIT Press.

Callon, M. 1986a. 'Some Elements of a Sociology of Translation: Domestication of the Scallops and the Fishermen of Saint Brieuc Bay', in *Power, Action and Belief: A New Sociology of Knowledge?* Sociological Review Monograph, edited by J. Law, 196–233. London: Routledge and Kegan Paul.

Callon, M. 1986b. 'The Sociology of an Actor-Network: The Case of the Electric Vehicle', in *Mapping the Dynamics of Science and Technology*, edited by M. Callon, J. Law and A. Rip, 19–34. Basingstoke: MacMillan.

Callon, M. 1996. 'Le travail de la conception en architecture', *Situations. Les Cahiers de la recherche architecturale* 37: 25–35.

Callon, M. and Law, J. 1995. 'Agency and the Hybrid Collectif', *The South Atlantic Quarterly* 94(2): 481–507.

Callon, M., Lascoumes, P. and Barthes, Y. 2011. 'Acting in an Uncertain World: An Essay on Technical Democracy', Translated by G. Burchell. Cambridge, MA: MIT Press.

Calvino, I. 1974. *Invisible Cities*. New York: Harcourt Brace Jovanovich.

Cavanagh, T., Verderber, S. and Oak A., eds., 2019. *Thinking While Doing: Explorations in Educational Design-Build*. Basel: Birkhäuser.

Crawshaw, J. 2021. *Art Worlding: Planning Relations*. Abingdon, UK: Routledge.

Cronon, W. 1991. *Nature's Metropolis. Chicago and the Great West*. New York, London: W. W. Norton and Company.

Cupers, K., ed., 2013. *Use Matters: An Alternative History of Architecture*. London: Routledge.

De Vries, G. 2016. *Bruno Latour* (Key Contemporary Thinkers). Cambridge: Polity.

Doucet, I. 2015. *The Practice Turn in Architecture: Brussels after 1968*. Farnham: Ashgate.

Easterling, K. 2012. 'We Will be Making Active Form', *Architectural Design* 82(5): 58–63.

Easterling, K. 2014. *Extrastatecraft: The Power of Infrastructure Space*. New York: Verso Books.

Evans, R. 1982. *The Fabrication of Virtue: English Prison Architecture, 1750–1840*. Cambridge: Cambridge University Press.

Farías, I. 2015. 'Epistemic Dissonance: Reconfiguring Valuation in Architectural Practice', in *Moments of Valuation: Exploring Sites of Dissonance*, edited by A. Berthoin Antal, M. Hutter and D. Stark, 271–289, Oxford: Oxford Scholarship Online.

Galison, P. and Thompson E., eds., 1999. *The Architecture of Science*. Cambridge, MA: The MIT Press.

Ghosn, R. and Jazairy, E. 2018. *Geostories: Another Architecture for the Environment*. NYC: Actar Publishers.

Ghosn, R., Jazairy, E. and Ramos S. 2008. 'The Space of Controversies: Interview with Bruno Latour', *New Geographies* 0: 122–135.

Gieryn, T. 2006. 'City as Truth-Spot: Laboratories and Field-sites in Urban Studies', *Social Studies of Science* 36(1): 5–38.

Gomart, E. and Hennion A. 1999. 'A Sociology of Attachment: Music Amateurs, Drug Users', in *Actor Network Theory and After*, edited by J. Law and J. Hassard, 220–248. Oxford: Blackwell.

Gottschling, P. 2015. 'To Submit is to Relate: A Study of Architectural Competitions within Networks of Practices', PhD Dissertation, University of Manchester.

Greimas, A.J. 1987. *On Meaning. Selected Writings in Semiotic Theory*. Minneapolis, MN: University of Minnesota Press.

Hansmann, S. 2021. *Monospace and Multiverse: Exploring Space with Actor-Network Theory*. Bielefeld: Transcript.

Harman. G. 2009. *Prince of Networks: Bruno Latour and Metaphysics*. Melbourne: Re: press.

Henderson, K. 1998. *On Line and On Paper: Visual Representations, Visual Culture, and Computer Graphics in Design Engineering*. Cambridge, MA: MIT Press.

Hennion, A. and Dubuisson, S. 1996. *Le Design: l'objet dans l'usage*. Paris: Presses des Mines.

Hill, J. 2003. *Actions of Architecture: Architects and Creative Users*. London: Routledge.

Houdart, S. and Minato, C. 2009. *Kuma Kengo. An Unconventional Monograph*. Paris: Editions Donner Lieu.

Jacobs, J.M. and Merriman P., eds., 2011. 'Practising Architecture', *Social and Cultural Geography* (special issue) 12(3).

Jacobs, J. M., Cairns, S. and Strebel, I. 2007. ' "A Tall Storey ..., but a Fact Just the Same": The Red Road High-rise as a Black Box', *Urban Studies* 44(3): 609–629.

James, W. 1996. *A Pluralistic Universe*. Lincoln: University of Nebraska Press.

Jaque, A. 2020. *The Superpower of Scale*. New York: Columbia University Press.

Jenkins, L. 2002. 'Geography and Architecture: 11, Rue du Conservatoire and the Permeability of Buildings', *Space and Culture* 5: 222–236.

Jensen, O.B. 2014. *Designing Mobilities*. Aalborg: Aalborg University Press.

Joerges, B. 1999. 'Do Politics Have Artefacts?' *Social Studies of Science* 29(3): 411–431.

Kärrholm, M. 2007. 'Materiality of Territorial Production: A Conceptual Discussion of Territoriality, Materiality, and the Everyday Life of Public Space', *Space & Culture* 4(10): 437–453.

Kärrholm, M. 2012. *Retailising Space: Architecture, Retail and the Territorialisation of Public Space*. Farnham: Ashgate.

King, A., ed., 1980. *Buildings and Society: Essays on the Social Development of the Built Environment*. London: Routledge & Kegan Paul.

Knorr-Cetina, K. 1981. *The Manufacture of Knowledge*. Oxford: Pergamon.

Koolhaas, R. 1978. *Delirious New York: a Retroactive Manifesto for Manhattan*. London: Thames and Hudson.

Koolhaas, R. and Latour, B. 'Dans Quel Monde Vivrons-Nous?' Filmed 26 January 2016 at L'Institut Français, Quai d'Orsay, Paris, France. Video, 50:11. Online. Available HTTP: <https://oma.eu/lectures/dans-quel-monde-vivrons-nous>, accessed 1 November, 2021.

Koolhaas, R., Mau, B., Sigler, J., Werlemann, H., and Office for Metropolitan Architecture. 1995. *Small, Medium, Large, Extra-large*. New York: Monacelli Press.

Kourri, D. 2022. 'Unfolding the Blanka Controversy: A Tunnel of Many Worlds', PhD Dissertation, University of Manchester.

Latour, B. 1987. *Science in Action: How to Follow Scientists and Engineers Through Society*. Cambridge, MA: Harvard University Press.

Latour, B. 1988a. *The Pasteurization of France*. Translated by A. Sheridan and J. Law. Cambridge, MA: Harvard University Press.

Latour, B. 1988b. 'The Politics of Explanation: An Alternative', in *Knowledge and Reflexivity: New Frontiers in the Sociology of Knowledge*, edited by S. Woolgar, 155–176. London: Sage.

Latour, B. 1991. 'The Berlin Key or How to Do things with Words', in *Matter, Materiality and Modern Culture*, edited by P.M. Graves-Brown, 10–21. London: Routledge.

Latour, B. 1992. 'Where Are the Missing Masses? The Sociology of a Few Mundane Artifacts', in *Shaping Technology/Building Society: Studies in Sociotechnical Change*, edited by W. Bijker and J. Law, 225–258, Cambridge, MA: MIT Press.

Latour, B. 1993a. *We Have Never Been Modern*. Translated by C. Porter. Cambridge: Harvard University Press.

Latour, B. 1993b. 'Ethnography of "High-tech": About the Aramis Case', in *Technological Choices – Transformations in Material Culture since the Neolithic*, edited by P. Lemonnier, 372–398. London: Routledge and Kegan Paul.

Latour, B. 1994. 'On Technical Mediation', *Common Knowledge* 3: 29–64.

Latour, B. 1995. 'Pasteur and Pouchet: The Heterogeneisis of the History of Science', in *History of Scientific Thought*, edited by M. Serres, 526–555. London: Blackwell.

Latour, B. 1996a. 'On Interobjectivity', *Mind, Culture, and Activity: An International Journal* 3(4): 228–245.

Latour, B. 1996b. *Aramis, or the Love of Technology*. Translated by C. Porter. Boston: Harvard University Press.

Latour, B. 1997. 'Trains of Thoughts – Piaget, Formalism and the Fifth Dimension', *Common Knowledge* 6(3): 170–191.

Latour, B. 1998. 'To modernize or to ecologize? That's the question', in *Remaking Reality: Nature at the Millennium*, edited by N. Castree and B. Willems-Braun, 221–242. London and New York: Routledge.

Latour, B. 1999a. 'Factures/Fractures: From the Concept of Network to the Concept of Attachment', *RES* 36: 20–32.

Latour, B. 1999b. *Pandora's Hope: An Essay on the Reality of Science Studies*. Cambridge, MA: Harvard University Press.

Latour, B. 2000. 'La Fin des Moyens', *Réseaux. Communication – Technologie – Société* 100: 39–58.

Latour, B. 2003. 'What if We Talked Politics a Little?', *Contemporary Political Theory* 2: 143–164.

Latour, B. 2004a. 'Why has Critique Run Out of Steam? From Matters of Fact to Matters of Concern', *Critical Inquiry* 30(2): 225–248.

Latour, B. 2004b. *Politics of Nature: How to Bring the Sciences into Democracy*. Translated by C. Porter. Cambridge, MA: Harvard University Press.

Latour, B. 2004c. 'Whose Cosmos, Which Cosmopolitics? Comments on the Peace Terms of Ulrich Beck', *Common Knowledge* 10(3): 450–462.

Latour, B. 2005a. 'En tapotant légèrement sur Rem Koolhas avec un bâton d'aveugle', *Architecture d'aujourd'hui*, 361: 70–79.

Latour, B. 2005b. *Reassembling the Social: An Introduction to Actor-Network-Theory*. Oxford: Oxford University Press.

Latour, B. 2005c. 'From Realpolitik to Dingpolitik: How to Make Things Public. An Introduction', in *Making Things Public: Atmospheres of Democracy*, edited by B. Latour and P. Weibel, 1–31. Cambridge, MA: MIT Press.

Latour, B. 2007a. 'The Recall of Modernity. Anthropological Approaches', *Cultural Studies Review* 13(1): 11–30.

Latour, B. 2007b. 'Is There Cosmopolitically Correct Design?' Lecture at the University of Manchester, Manchester Architecture Research Centre, 5 October.

Latour, B. 2008. 'Where Are the Missing Masses? The Sociology of a Few Mundane Artefacts', in *Technology and Society, Building Our Sociotechnical Future*, edited by D.J. Johnson, and J.M. Wetmore, 151–180. Cambridge, MA: MIT Press.

Latour, B. 2010a. *The Making of Law: An Ethnography of the Conseil d'Etat*. Translated by M. Brilman and A. Pottage. Cambridge: Polity Press.

Latour, B. 2010b. 'An Attempt at a "Compositionist Manifesto"', *New Literary History* 41: 471–490.

Latour, B. 2010c. *On the Modern Cult of the Factish Gods*. Durham, NC: Duke University Press.

Latour, B. 2011. 'Paris, Invisible City: The Plasma', *City, Culture and Society (CCS)* 2(4): 91–93.

Latour, B. 2013. *Rejoicing: Or the Torments of Religious Speech*. Cambridge: Polity Press.

Latour, B. 2015. 'Waiting for Gaia. Composing the Common World through Arts and Politics', in *What is Cosmopolitical Design? Design, Nature and the Built Environment*, edited by A. Yaneva and A. Zaera-Polo, 21–33. New York: Routledge.

Latour, B. 2017a. *Facing Gaia. Eight Lectures on the New Climatic Regime*. Translated by C. Porter. London: Polity Press.

Latour, B. 2017b. 'Why Gaia is not a God of Totality', *Theory, Culture and Society* 34: 61–82.

Latour, B. 2018a. 'On a Possible Triangulation of Some Present Political Positions', *Critical Inquiry* 44: 213–226.

Latour, B. 2018b. *Down to Earth: Politics in the New Climatic Regime*. Translated by C. Porter. London: Polity Press.

Latour, B. 2020. 'What Protective Measures Can You Think Of So We Don't Go Back to the Pre-crisis Production Model?', *AOC*, 29 March, 2020. Online. Available HTTP: <https://aoc.media/opinion/2020/03/29/imaginer-les-gestes-barrieres-contre-le-retour-a-la-production-davant-crise/>, accessed 15 November, 2020.

Latour, B. and Hermant, E. 1998. *Paris, Ville Invisible*. Paris: Les empêcheurs de penser en rond/La Découverte.

Latour, B. and Hermant, E. 1998. *Paris, The Invisible City*. Translated by L. Libbrecht. Online. Available HTTP: <http://www.bruno-latour.fr/virtual/index.html>, accessed 1 November, 2021.

Latour, B. and Lenton, T.M. 2019. 'Extending the Domain of Freedom, or Why Gaia is So Hard to Understand', *Critical Inquiry* 45: 659–680.

Latour, B. and Weibel, P., eds., 2005. *Making Things Public: Atmospheres of Democracy*. Cambridge, MA: MIT Press.

Latour B. and Weibel, P., 2020. *Critical Zones: The Science and Politics of Landing on Earth*. Cambridge, MA: MIT Press.

Latour, B. and Woolgar, S. 1979. *Laboratory Life: The Social Construction of Scientific Facts*, second edition. Los Angeles: Sage.

Latour, B. and Yaneva, A. 2008. 'Give Me a Gun and I will Make All Buildings Move: An ANT's View of Architecture', in *Explorations in Architecture: Teaching, Design, Research*, edited by R. Geiser, 89–89. Basel: Birkhäuser.

Lefebvre, P. 2018. 'I, T.T. Stands. Two Days in the Life of an Object in the Making', *Ardeth* 1(2): 97–119.

Llach, D. 2015. *Buildings of the Vision: Software and the Imagination of Design*. London, UK: Routledge.

Loukissas, Y. 2012. *Co-Designers: Cultures of Computer Simulation in Architecture*. UK: Routledge.

Lovell, S. 2017. *Berlin in Fifty Design Icons*. London: Hachette UK.

Lynch, M. 1985. *Art and Artifact in Laboratory Science: A Study of Shop Work and Shop Talk in a Research Laboratory*. London: Routledge & Kegan Paul.

Mauz, I. and Gravelle J. 2005. 'Wolves in the Valley: on Making a Controversy Public', in *Making Things Public*, edited by B. Latour and P. Wiebel, 370–380. Karlsruhe: ZKM/Cambridge: MIT Press.

Mitchell, S. 2022. 'Rethinking Bauhaus Architectural Heritage: Logics of Valuation Through Collecting, Archiving, and Exhibiting', PhD Dissertation, University of Manchester.

Mommersteeg, B. 2020. 'Variations of a Building: An Ontological Politics of Architecture', PhD Dissertation, University of Manchester.

Moore, S. and Wilson, B. 2013. *Questioning Architectural Judgement. The Problem of Codes in the United States*. London: Routledge.

Murphy, K.M. 2015. *Swedish Design: An Ethnography*. Ithaca, NY: Cornell University.

Novoselov, K. and Yaneva, A. 2020. *The New Architecture of Science: Learning from Graphene*. Singapore and NYC: World Scientific Publishing.

Ohanian, M., and Royoux, J-C., eds., 2004. *Cosmograms*. New York: Lukas & Sternberg.

Pickering, A. 1992. *Science as Practice and Culture*. Chicago: University of Chicago Press.

Rose, G., Degen M. and Basdas, B. 2010. 'More on "Big Things": Building Events and Feelings', *Transactions of the Institute of British Geographers* 35: 334–349.

Rose, G., Degen M. and Mehuish, C. 2014. 'Networks, Interfaces and Computer-Generated Images: Learning form Digital Visualisations of Urban Redevelopment Projects', *Environment and Planning D: Society and Space* 32(3): 386–403.

Ross, L. 2022. *Pyrotechnic Cities: Architecture, Fire-Safety & Standardisation.* Abingdon, UK: Routledge.

Schmidgen, H. 2014. *Bruno Latour in Pieces: An Intellectual Biography.* New York: Fordham University Press.

Shapin, S. and Schaffer, S. 1985. *Leviathan and the Air-Pump: Hobbes, Boyle, and the Experimental Life.* Princeton, N.J.: Princeton University Press.

Sharif, A. 2016. 'Sustainable Architectural Design between Inscription and De-scription: The Case of Masdar City', PhD Dissertation, University of Manchester.

Shayya, F. 2021. 'Politics of Survivability: How Military Technology Scripts Urban Relations', PhD Dissertation, University of Manchester.

Simondon, G. 1989. *Du mode d'existence des objets techniques, (réédition avec postface et préface).* Paris: Aubier.

Sloterdijk, P. 2005. 'Foreword to the Theory of Spheres', in *Cosmograms*, edited by M. Ohanian and J.C. Royoux, 223–241. New York: Lukas and Sternberg.

Sloterdijk, P. 2016. *Globes: Foams: Spheres Volume III: Plural Spherology.* Translated by W. Hoban. Los Angeles: Semiotext(e).

Sorkin, M. 2009. *Twenty Minutes in Manhattan.* New York: Reaktion books.

Stengers, I. 2005. 'The Cosmopolitical Proposal', in *Making Things Public: Atmospheres of Democracy*, edited by B. Latour and Weibel, P. 994–1003. Cambridge: MIT Press.

Stengers, I. 2010a. *Cosmopolitics I.* Translated by Robert Bononno. Minneapolis: Minnesota University Press.

Stengers, I. 2010b. *Cosmopolitics II.* Translated by Robert Bononno. Minneapolis: Minnesota University Press.

Stengers, I. 2015. *In Catastrophic Times: Resisting the Coming Barbarism.* Translated by Andrew Goffey. London: Open Humanities Press.

Stengers, I. 2018. *Another Science is Possible: A Manifesto for Slow Science.* Translated by Stephen Muecke. Cambridge, UK: Polity Press.

Strebel, I. 2011. 'The Living Building: Towards a Geography of Maintenance Work', *Social & Cultural Geography* 12(3): 243–262.

Strum, S. and Latour, B. 1987. 'Redefining the Social Link: from Baboons to Humans', *Social Science Information* 26(4): 783–802.

Till, J. 2009. *Architecture Depends*. Cambridge, MA: MIT Press.

Tresch, J. 2005. 'Cosmogram', in *Cosmogram*, edited by J-C. Royoux and M. Ohanian, 67–76. Berlin: Sternberg Press.

Tresch, J. 2007. 'Technological World-Pictures. Cosmic Things and Cosmograms', *Isis* 98(1): 84–99.

Venturini, T. 2010. 'Building on Faults: How to Represent Controversies with Digital Methods', *Public Understanding of Science* 21(7): 796–812.

Vinck, D., ed., 2003. *Everyday Engineering: An Ethnography of Design and Innovation*. Cambridge, MA: MIT Press.

Watts, J. 2020. 'Bruno Latour: "This is a global catastrophe that has come from within" ', *The Guardian*, 6 June, 2020. Online. Available HTTP: <https://www.theguardian.com/world/2020/jun/06/bruno-latour-coronavirus-gaia-hypothesis-climate-crisis>, accessed 1 November, 2021.

Winner, L. 1980. 'Do Artefacts have Politics?' *Daedalus* 109(1): 121–136.

Yaneva, A. 1997. 'Microanalyse de la forme sociale des objets techniques: sur les modes d'emploi des robots', mémoire de DEA en Sociologie, EHESS, Paris.

Yaneva, A. 2001. 'L'affluence des objets: pragmatique comparée de l'art contemporain et de l'artisanat d'art', Doctoral Thesis, l'Ecole Nationale Supérieure des mines de Paris.

Yaneva, A. 2005. 'Scaling up and Down: Extraction Trials in Architectural Design', *Social Studies of Science* 35: 867–894.

Yaneva, A. 2009a. 'Making the Social Hold: Towards an Actor-Network Theory of Design', *Design and Culture* 1(3): 273–288.

Yaneva, A. 2009b. *Made by the Office for Metropolitan Architecture. An Ethnography of Design*. Rotterdam: 010 Publishers.

Yaneva, A. 2009c. *The Making of a Building: A Pragmatist Approach to Architecture*. Oxford: Peter Lang.

Yaneva, A. 2010. 'The Architectural as a Type of Connector.' *Perspecta, The Yale Architectural Journal* 42: 138–143.

Yaneva, A., ed., 2011. 'Traceable Cities', *City, Culture and Society (CCS)* (special issue) 2(4): 87–89.

Yaneva, A. 2012. *Mapping Controversies in Architecture*. Farnham: Ashgate.

Yaneva, A. 2017. *Five Ways to Make Architecture Political. An Introduction to the Politics of Design Practice*. London: Bloomsbury.

Yaneva, A. 2018. 'New Voices in Architectural Ethnography', Editorial. *Ardeth* (Architectural Design Theory) 1(2): 17–35.

Yaneva, A. 2020. *Crafting History: Archiving and the Quest for Architectural Legacy*. London, UK: Cornell University Press.

Yaneva, A. and Heaphy, L. 2012. 'Urban Controversies and the Making of the Social', *Architectural Research Quarterly* 16(1): 29–36.

Yaneva, A. and Hennion, A. 2000. *Savoirs rares, objets de qualité, artisanats d'exception: définir la qualité pour la maintenir et la produire, rapport du CSI*, Ecole nationale supérieure des mines de Paris, Paris.

Yaneva, A. and Mommersteeg, B. 2019. 'How does an ANT approach help us rethink the notion of site?', in *The Routledge Companion to Actor-Network Theory*, edited by A. Blok, I. Farías and C. Roberts, 306–317. London: Routledge.

Yaneva, A. and Zaera-Polo, A., eds., 2015. *What is Cosmopolitical Design? Design, Nature and the Built Environment*. New York: Routledge.

Yarrow, T. 2019 *Architects: Portraits of a Practice*. Ithaca, NY: Cornell University Press.

Zitouni, B. 2010. *Agglomérer. Une anatomie de l'extension bruxelloise (1828–1915)*. Brussels: VUBPRESS.

Index

actant 28–29, 83, 85–86
Actor-Network Theory 1–3, 63–65, 125
actor-network 66, 71
agency 22, 29, 55–56, 62, 112, 116, 120
Akrich, Madeleine 2, 43–44, 48–49, 52
ANT *see* Actor-Network Theory 1–2, 54, 64–76
Anthropocene 114–115, 117, 120–121
anthropology of science 3, 36; symmetrical anthropology 13, 36, 58
associations 24, 27, 29–30, 32–33, 35, 38, 40, 42, 49, 66, 70, 72, 85, 103, 113–114

black box 26, 50
Bourdieu, Pierre 24
Boyle, Robert 6, 106

Callon, Michel 2, 23, 43–44, 55, 69, 108
capitalism 29, 32
Centre de Sociologie de l'Innovation (CSI) 2, 43
chains of translation 32, 34
climate change 3, 113, 121, 125
climatic regime 3, 114–115, 120–121
collective(s) 11, 27, 55, 67, 106, 110–111
constitution *see* modern Constitution 5–7, 13; non-modern Constitution 12

constructivism 69; social constructivism 56, 69
cosmogram 114, 122–123
cosmopolitics 109–110, 112
cosmos 106, 109–114, 121
critical project 10
critical theory 46
critique 3, 6, 11, 24, 39, 46, 64
culture vs. nature 5–7, 9–15, 38, 87, 110, 113, 116

diffusion model 31–32, 34
Dingpolitik 107
discovery 30, 117

ecology 1, 9, 74, 113
engineers 8, 12, 20, 23, 30, 32–33, 36, 48, 52, 57–58, 60, 82, 104, 110–111
epistemology 40; political epistemology 106
ethics 52, 55
event 18–19, 21, 24, 71, 78, 81–82, 85, 93

factish 76
Foucault, Michel 91

Gaia 115–121, 123–124
globalisation 1, 16, 115, 118–119, 125

globe 115, 118–119, 121–122, 124
Greimas, A. J. 28–29

Hobbes, Thomas 6, 106
Hobbes vs. Boyles 6, 106
hybridisation 10, 18–19
hybrid(s) 9–11, 13, 15, 55, 108–109, 112

immutable mobiles 27, 83
infra-language 65
innovation 1–3, 32, 43, 57, 68
inscription 27–28, 32, 38; inscription devices 27–28
institution 28, 56, 58, 74–75, 96, 113,
interobjectivity 100–101
intersubjectivity 100
irreduction 86

James, William 111

Kelvin, Lord 69–71
knowledge production 1

L'Ecole Nationale Supérieure des Mines de Paris 2
Laboratory Life 20–21, 24, 36
laboratory 6, 21, 23, 28, 34, 69
law 6, 9, 36–38, 94, 119
Law, John 55, 125
Lovelock, James 116–117

machines 20–21, 31–32, 55, 59, 61, 86
Making of Law 36–37
mapping 3, 39–40, 95, 121, 124

mapping controversies 39–42
Margulis, Lynn 116–117
Marx, Karl 24, 63
matters of concern 70, 107–108, 110
matters of fact 21–22, 70, 108
mediation 11–12, 15, 18, 32, 43, 71, 76, 80, 83, 85,
mediator 50–51, 68–71, 74–75, 77, 82, 101, 106–107
metrology 92, 101
micro and macro 63, 71, 97–98
modern Constitution 5–7, 13
modernity 1, 3, 5–7, 9–11, 13, 15, 17, 105
modernisation 5, 16, 113, 118–120
morality 48, 52, 55
morally responsible 115

network *see* actor-network 9–10, 15, 24, 34–35, 50, 53, 57, 59, 69–72, 78, 82, 86–87, 92–94, 97, 100–102, 104, 107, 109, 112, 114
negotiation 22, 33, 56, 59, 81, 108
nonhuman actors 59
non-modern 11–13, 16, 78, 111
non-modern Constitution 12

object-oriented politics 107–109
oligopticon 91–98, 100, 102–104

panopticon 91, 93
panorama 89–90
parliament of things 105–107
Pasteur, Louis 30, 66, 106
Pasteurization of France 86

139   INDEX

pluriverse 110
political ecology 1, 113
Politics of Nature 117
postmodernism 11, 17–18
principle of symmetry 11, 33
programme of action 39, 46–48, 53, 55, 100; anti-programme 47–48, 53–54
purification 9

quasi-object 58

Reassembling the Social 64, 101
relativism 35, 58, 70
relativity 70, 87
religion 1, 117
representation 7, 28, 35, 48, 62, 103, 107–108, 121–122

Science in Action 20, 24
science studies *see* STS 24, 28, 40, 122
scientists 6, 9, 15, 20–24, 27, 30, 32–34, 38–39, 63, 65, 72, 107, 111–112

semiotics 28, 40
Sloterdijk, Peter 122, 125
social constructivism 56, 69
social sciences 20, 40, 64, 70, 102, 110, 112
sociology 1–2, 22, 24–26, 29, 33, 38, 46–47, 49, 54, 56, 63, 70, 76, 92, 102; sociology of associations 70
spacing 3, 79, 82–85, 87
Stengers, Isabelle 95, 109–110, 113, 124
Strum, Shirley 63
STS 2
symbols 46, 49, 56, 75, 102

technoscience 34–35
translation 9–12, 15, 19, 27, 30–34, 36, 53, 55, 60, 66, 70–71, 85
translation model 30–32, 36

Whitehead, Alfred North 18
Woolgar, Steve 20–23

For Product Safety Concerns and Information please contact our EU
representative GPSR@taylorandfrancis.com
Taylor & Francis Verlag GmbH, Kaufingerstraße 24, 80331 München, Germany